Small Isles

*Eigg, Canna, Rum and Muck

The authors and publisher have made every effort to ensure that the information in this publication is accurate, and accept no responsibility whatsoever for any loss, injury or inconvenience experienced by any person or persons whilst using this book.

published by
pocket mountains ltd
The Old Church, Annanside,
Moffat DG10 9HB

ISBN: 978-1-907025-71-6

Text and photography copyright © Paul and Helen Webster 2019

The right of Paul and Helen Webster to be identified as the Authors of this work has been asserted by them in accordance with the Copyright, Designs and Patents Act 1988

A catalogue record for this book is available from the British Library

Contains Ordnance Survey data © Crown copyright and database 2019 supported by out of copyright mapping 1945-1961

Printed in Poland

Ferry arriving at Eigg ▶

Introduction

The Small Isles and their neighbours Coll and Tiree provide a remarkable range of walking, wildlife-watching and photography opportunities – all combined with that special indefinable island magic. Many visitors claim they breathe a sigh of relief as they step off the ferry, leaving behind their mainland cares to instead sink into 'island time' – becoming a temporary member of one of these tiny communities.

Rum, Eigg, Canna and Muck are the main islands that make up the Small Isles which in turn form part of the disparate Inner Hebrides archipelago off the west coast of Scotland. Each island has its own unique character, reflected in the type of walks on offer there. Rum boasts one of

Scotland's most dramatic mountain ranges, and its wild hinterland is home to a large and much-studied red deer population. Eigg is thriving since its community buyout in 1997; it has the largest population, and here the walks explore its extraordinary geology, including the iconic rock peak of the Sgurr of Eigg, large sea caves and fine sandy beaches. Canna is a green gem where fine coastal cliffs and seabird colonies vie for the walker's attention. Muck is the smallest of the islands, its mix of emerald fields and varied coastline offering a complete escape from mainstream tourism. The Calmac ferry plies between all four isles from Mallaig, its timetable providing endless

permutations for island-hopping trips.

Further south are the larger islands of Coll and Tiree, accessed by car ferry from Oban. Both are fairly low-lying and blessed with some of Scotland's finest sandy beaches and are known for their sunny climate, but they too are distinct in character. Rugged Coll's wild interior is studded with low, rocky hills and secluded sandy coves. More fertile with a larger resident population, Tiree has earned fame as a mecca for surfers and windsurfers.

Whichever island you choose to visit first, once you've been bitten by the island-bagging bug it will become impossible to resist the lure of sampling another of these Scottish island gems.

How to use this guide

This book contains 36 walks providing a sample of the best adventures on foot for each island. Many are on paths, tracks and minor roads; check the 'Terrain' (at the top of each route) to see if the ground is

Balephuil Bay on Tiree ▼

likely to be boggy, particularly steep or rocky. Bear in mind that ground conditions can be as changeable as the weather and take appropriate footwear.

A sketch map accompanies each route: however, apart from very short trails, it is essential to have an Ordnance Survey (OS) map with you in case you stray off the route or need to find a shortcut to safety. You should pack waterproofs on all but the shortest walks, and the more mountainous routes such as Hallival, Orval or the Sgurr require full hillwalking gear. Some routes can become somewhat overgrown with bracken in the high summer but should usually be passable.

Access and safety

The Land Reform (Scotland) Act 2003 gave walkers the right of access over most Scottish land away from residential buildings. With these rights come responsibilities as set out in the Scottish Access Code, which basically comes down

to showing respect for other land users and acting responsibly. On the islands, this would mean, in particular, taking note of any livestock on farmed and grazing land, keeping dogs under tight control and away from livestock at all times and ensuring they do not disturb any groundnesting birds in the spring and early summer. (For more information on the Scottish Outdoor Access Code check www.outdooraccess-scotland.scot.)

Deer stalking takes place on Rum between 1 July and 20 October, but should not conflict with any of the routes in this guide. As always pay heed to any local diversions or signs about forestry operations, local closures and wildlife.

Midges can sometimes be a problem on the more sheltered Small Isles (the breeze tends to keep them at bay on Coll and Tiree) with Rum being most notorious in the summer months – long sleeves, a midge net and insect repellent will be your friends – and possibly a midgie coil or citronella candle to burn in the evenings if camping.

Ticks are potentially a more serious problem and can be encountered wherever there are sheep and deer. Wear light-coloured long trousers and tuck them in if you are prone to ticks, and check yourself every evening, using a tick remover or tweezers to get rid of them. Some insect repellents can also help stop them from attaching themselves to you.

Getting here

The Small Isles are served by daily ferries from Mallaig (connected by train from Fort William and Glasgow) – permits for cars are only issued to island dwellers. Carefully studying of the timetable is required as trips are not possible to each island on every day and landing times vary. The MV *Sheerwater* runs out of Arisaig daily in the summer months, making a variety of landings and cruises around the Small Isles. It is also possible for experienced kayakers and boaters to reach the islands, all of which have moorings for visiting yachts.

Coll and Tiree are reached by daily vehicle ferries from Oban (train and bus connections to Glasgow), taking approximately 2 hours 30 to Coll and three hours to Tiree (via Coll). Hebridean Air Services runs a twice-weekly service to both the islands from Oban with additional flights in the summer. Charter boats will also make the journey, as can expert kayakers and boat owners.

As will all island journeys it's best to be prepared for disruption. The weather can change rapidly and often causes ferry and flight delays or cancellations.

History

These islands haven't always seemed so remote – in the past, the seas around them were the main thoroughfares for travel and they were in prime position both strategically and for providing a viable place to farm and fish. There is

View from An Sgurr on Eigg ▶

evidence of early man on all of the islands, including carved Celtic crosses, Iron Age souterrains and early forts and castles. More recently the islands supported relatively large populations that were dependent on crofting, fishing and, in the 18th century, harvesting and processing kelp. The tide of depopulation on the islands began when the kelp industry collapsed, in combination with potato famines, industrialisation and forced clearances by landlords to make way for sheep. Emigration and work opportunities in the growing Scottish cities saw communities continue to shrink. More recently the islands have been fighting back to reverse this with community buyouts, as well as a growth in new crofts, tourism and other businesses that have lured both new and returning families to seek to make a living here.

Accommodation

Options to stay on all these islands have expanded in the last few years, with the number of bunkhouses and glamping-type accommodation, in particular, on the up. Self-catering, bed and breakfast and more basic hostel-type accommodation complements the existing camping offering – but it's best to book ahead, especially in the summer months or if your trip coincides with a local event such as the Tiree Wave Classic or the music festivals on Eigg or Tiree.

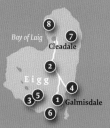

Loch Scresort
Kinloch

R u m

Sound of Rum

The massive rock prow of An Sgurr is a remarkable sight, making Eigg instantly recognisable whether seen from the sea or from Morar's silver sands. Formed from a volcanic eruption on Rum, the island packs great variety into a small space. A history of absentee and eccentric landlords combined with high-handed treatment of tenants had led to bitter resentment within Eigg's community, which was eventually resolved with a community buyout in 1997. Intense media scrutiny into a community often feted as exemplar by land reform advocates has sometimes led to tension, but overall Eigg has gone from strength to strength since then with a growing population, new ferry jetty and renewable energy, forestry and tourism schemes all adding to the traditional crofting life of the island.

Today there is a wide variety of accommodation available, as well as an informal campsite. A well-stocked shop and café/bar operate year round. Bikes are useful on the island – you can bring your own on the ferry or hire one here – but not essential; a quiet road from the pier links to Cleadale at the far end of the island, which has the most fertile croftland, as well as fabulous beaches

Bay of Laig
Cleadale

E i g g

Galmisdale

Sound of Eigg

M u c k

Port Mor

looking over to Rum. Close to the ferry pier you can explore two large caves, one once used for worship whilst the other has a grim history of clan massacre. A more peaceful stroll takes in the grounds of the Lodge, some sheltered beaches and the woods of Galmisdale.

A r d n a m u r c h a n

Eigg

Lodge and Manse circular

Distance 3.75km Time 2 hours
Terrain rough tracks, minor road and
clear paths; burn crossing on stones
Map OS Explorer 397 Access ferry to Eigg
pier from Mallaig, limited summer
service from Arisaig

This short walk explores the sheltered
area of Galmisdale from Eigg's ferry pier.
It passes through woods to reach the
colonial-style lodge house before a more
open section leads past the old Manse
and down to the shore, returning by
the old harbour.

Start from the Am Laimhrig building at
the end of the ferry jetty which houses
the island shop, café and toilets. Continue
up the road, passing to the left of the
standing stone and wigwam camping
pods overlooking the bay and natural
harbour. The road soon becomes a track,
passing a house and then turning right

through stone gateposts onto the
driveway of the Lodge, passing the
community hall on your left.

You soon come to the Lodge. This
elegant neo-colonial building was
constructed in the 1920s for the shipping
magnate Sir Walter Runciman who owned
Eigg from 1922 until 1966 when it was sold
to another largely absentee landlord. Less
than a decade later, a new owner arrived,
businessman, powerboat racer and
bobsleigh enthusiast, Keith Schellenberg,
who made this his main residence on
the island. Schellenberg fell out with
many of the residents over lack of
investment, his alleged high-handed
management and habit of driving across
the island in a Silver Shadow Rolls Royce
(later mysteriously destroyed in a fire).
He eventually sold the island on to a
German pop artist.

Following the islanders' acquisition of

◄ Kayaking off Eigg

the Lodge as part of a community buyout, it was deemed too expensive and unsustainable for the island trust to renovate, having fallen almost to dereliction. Eventually the listed building was bought by newcomers to the island; it has been partially restored and currently hosts eco- and yoga courses, as well as offering accommodation.

The gardens were largely planted in the 1930s and the surviving azaleas, eucalyptus, palms and flame trees are testament to the warming effect of the Gulf Stream and the sheltered location. Head straight past the Lodge, following the track as it curves right. Go through a gate onto open ground, bearing right at a fork to head downhill. After passing some huts, you soon reach Eigg's 'main road' where you turn left to rise gently uphill, passing an old postbox and Manse Wood on your right. Turn right across a high wooden stile over a wall to take a faint path across the field, aiming for the large Manse. Built in 1790 in the style of a Georgian farmhouse, it was later enlarged. After selling the island in 1995, Schellenberg hung onto the Manse; the house fell into

disrepair but following a change of ownership it has been restored.

Cross another stile just before the Manse and bear right, keeping to the right of the garden wall. Follow a faint path curving downhill to another stile over a fence with a view ahead to Eilean Chathastail and the ferry pier. The route soon joins a grassy track, still aiming downhill and staying to the left of a drystane dyke. Eventually, after passing through a gate, aim diagonally right across a grassy area to meet a burn that flows into the sea. Cross at the stepping stones and take the path around the shore, passing the old harbour and shortly emerging at the road. Turn left to pass Shore Cottage and reach the start.

11

The road to Laig Bay

Distance 12.4km **Time** 4 hours
Terrain minor road, beach, paths very
boggy in places **Map** OS Explorer 397
Access ferry to Eigg pier from Mallaig,
limited summer service from Arisaig

**Cross Eigg on its only road to Laig Bay
where the stunning sands offer a
fabulous view of the Isle of Rum.
The return walk climbs across croftland
and meanders through forestry to return
to the pier.**

   Start by forking right from the pier and
walking along the shore road, crossing
the cattle grid and passing beneath the
community-run wigwams. Pass the two
cottages at the sheltered bay and
continue up the road, using the bypass
path to cut the corner on the ascent. After
the road levels off it passes a large
standing stone. Originally one of the

pitchstone lava columns of An Sgurr, it is
thought to be one in a line of ancient
pillar crosses once set throughout the
island. It was re-erected in the 1990s by
residents as a symbol of their resistance
to absentee landlords.

   Ignore the road off to the right, which
leads to Kildonan, and pass the primary
school. With a population of around 100
the primary school has a handful of
pupils, a nursery and two teachers with a
shared headteacher also overseeing the
school on Muck. Secondary school-age
children can be educated in Mallaig with
local families providing board during the
week. Just beyond the school is the Old
Shop; once Scotland's smallest co-
operative it now houses a fascinating
display about the island's natural and
built heritage.

   Keep heading along the road as it

Cleadale

Bay of
Laig

Cuagach

◀ Isle of Rum from Laig Bay

Laig

heritage
centre

school

shed

Kildonan

The Manse

Sandamhor

Poll nam
Partan

The Lodge

Galmisdale

Eilean
Chathastail

0   1km

begins to descend towards the fertile croftland at Cleadale and passes a few houses at Cuagach. After a sharp bend take the second track on the left, opposite an old postbox, aiming towards the church – if you get to the fork in the road at the war memorial you have gone too far. The track leads down to the beach, passing a small wooden house with a stunning view out over the water. The dramatic mountains of the Rum Cuillin are often reflected on the wet sand – the sunsets from here are renowned.

Bear left across the sands, crossing a burn part way along (cross near the outflow on the beach or further upstream if the water is high), and take the track heading towards the buildings at Laig, passing a small holiday house overlooking the bay. Walk past some farm buildings and when the track leads right up to the farmhouse turn off onto a lower track on the left. This soon crosses a burn on a footbridge and passes one of the island's hydro-electric buildings. As the route climbs there are good views down onto the lochan which is surrounded by native bluebells in late spring.

After a gate the route squeezes between rock walls to reach the crest of the hill and then follows an indistinct trail over very boggy, heathery ground – keep the trees

on your left. Eventually the path meets a track; turn right here and when you reach a large shed, keep left to head uphill. Carry straight on at a junction, with the route soon narrowing to a path with marker posts. As the path descends there are views to the sea ahead and, after a gate, you emerge at the road. Turn right to return to the start at the pier.

Ruins of Grulin

**Distance 6.7km Time 2 hours 30 to 3 hours
Terrain farm track and grassy path
Map OS Explorer 397 Access ferry to Eigg
pier from Mallaig, limited summer
service from Arisaig**

A track strikes out across the moors in
the shadow of the great southern face of
An Sgurr to visit the ruins of Grulin.
This cleared settlement is set amongst
massive boulders above the sea – a truly
atmospheric spot.

From the pier, shop and café building
head up the road, passing to the left of
the standing stone that commemorates
the community buyout of the island in
1997. The road becomes a track and,
after a house, passes the entrance to the
Lodge and a green building which is the
community hall – host to many a
legendary ceilidh night. Ignore a track on
the left (this leads eventually to the caves)
and continue to a gate. Pass through this
and cross the field ahead, aiming directly
for the crofthouse with the great looming
prow of An Sgurr behind.

Once close to Galmisdale House stay on
the track which bends right to reach a
gate. Go through this and turn left on the
track beyond. Ignore the path off to the

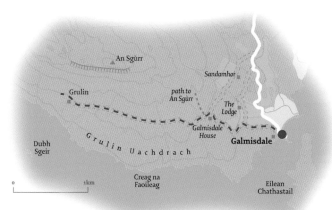

An Sgùrr

Sandamhor

Grulin

path to
An Sgùrr

The
Lodge

Galmisdale
House

Galmisdale

Dubh
Sgeir

G r u l i n   U a c h d r a c h

0   1km

Creag na
Faoileag

Eilean
Chathastail

right for An Sgurr, instead remaining on the track. This climbs gently, passing a cairn marking the spot where coffin bearers rested during the funeral procession of a famed Grulin piper. Over to your left are the wind turbines that form part of Eigg's electricity network. Although most of the power is generated from a number of small-scale hydro schemes, wind and solar also help to make the island self-sufficient in energy, having switched from diesel generators following the community buyout. Use of electricity is limited, but residents say that the supply is more than adequate for family households if usage is monitored and spread throughout the day.

As the track progresses there are good views south over to the Isle of Muck, whilst the great cliffs of An Sgurr dominate to the north. Fork right to pass

in front of a restored cottage, the only building still standing in Grulin, and continue ahead to explore the rest of the ruins set amongst some impressively large boulders dragged here by retreating glaciers in the last ice age. Records show that in 1841 there were 103 islanders living at Grulin but by the early 1850s the grazing land had been let to a sheep farmer from the Borders who forcibly cleared the village, keeping one family on as shepherd. In total 14 families were forced to leave in 1853, most emigrating to Nova Scotia where there are a number of settlements with names from Eigg.

Once you have explored the area, perhaps searching out the Well of the Holy Women, a spring surrounded by stones on a slope heading towards the cliff edge, the return is by the same outward route.

◀ Restored cottage at Grulin

Kildonan shore walk

Distance 6.25km Time 2 hours
Terrain minor road, rough tracks and
paths Map OS Explorer 397
Access ferry to Eigg pier from Mallaig,
limited summer service from Arisaig

Follow the coastline from Eigg's ferry
pier to enjoy stunning views, sandy bays
and the chance to look for otters from
a rocky headland.

Start from the shop and café building
near the pier at Galmisdale Bay and take
the road along the shore, passing below
the wigwams and standing stone. Soon it
leads past a couple of cottages; beyond
these, before the road starts to climb, turn
right onto a track leading past the old
harbour. Whilst a safe anchorage, this bay
remains inaccessible to boats at
low tides, so the new long jetty
allowing direct access to roll-on
roll-off ferries has been a huge
boon to the island community.

The track passes through a rock cutting
and then rounds the bay to reach a grassy
area which also operates as the island's
informal camping ground. Cross the burn
on the stepping stones and carry on along
the shore – or enjoy the sands at low tide.
Behind you, the Sgurr of Eigg looms over
the island looking completely unreal.

Stay on the grass as you follow the
shore; there are occasional orange
markers. After rounding the small
headland to overlook the next bay you
can detour down a small path to the ruins
of a cliffside house, but it's necessary to
retrace your steps from here as there is no
way through. From the cliff above the
ruins head uphill and inland for a short
way to reach a gate. Go through this and
follow a grassy track until markers
indicate where to swing right to reach a
fence. Walk alongside this until you come
to a stile overlooking the bay.

Once over the stile, descend the steep

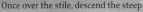

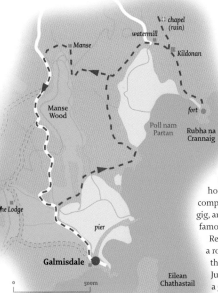

Manse
watermill
chapel
(ruin)
Kildonan
fort
Manse
Wood
Poll nam
Partan
Rubha na
Crannaig
the Lodge
pier
Galmisdale
Eilean
Chathastail
0   500m

raids, the monastery was abandoned and St Donnan went to Iona. There is a fine carved cross – now in a couple of pieces– and it is worth continuing a little further up the hill to see the chapel itself which houses an enigmatic carving, compared by some to a sheela-na-gig, and a burial plaque to a famous Eigg piper.

Return to the track, soon taking a rough path just to the right of the house and garden fence. Just past the house go through a gate and, keeping to the dry higher ground as far as possible, aim for the rocky headland, passing a prominent chambered cairn along the way. At the shore is a stunning sandy beach at low tide, a great spot for a picnic or some otter sleuthing amidst the kelp.

To return, head back along the road and then the shore path on the left after the mill. Once back at the stile at the clifftop, keep straight ahead over grass and then bear right on a grassy track. Cross a stile and pass in front of the large Manse ahead, crossing another stile to the left to take a faint path above Manse Wood. Keep below a house on the right to soon reach a tall stile at the road. Turn left to follow this road back to the pier.

path which leads down through trees at the base of the cliffs to shortly emerge onto a road at a gate. Turn right to pass Kildonan Mill. This was built for the landowner who then charged the locals to grind their corn and oats; he set about destroying all the quernstones on the island so that there was no alternative to using, and paying for, the mill.

Before you arrive at the gate to Kildonan House, a small sign directs you left for a detour up to the ruined chapel and graveyard. Here, in the 7th century, St Donnan established a very early monastery which at one time housed more than 50 monks. Following Viking

◀ The broken cross at Kildonan

The Sgurr of Eigg

**Distance 8km Time 3 to 4 hours (return)
Terrain boggy path, steep with some
minor rocky scrambling, occasional red
waymarkers Map OS Explorer 397
Access ferry to Eigg pier from Mallaig,
limited summer service from Arisaig**

**The massive prow of An Sgurr dominates
Eigg and looks impossibly steep and
intimidating. However, the ascent route
winds around the far side to provide a
rough but fairly straightforward hillwalk
to this very dramatic summit.**

Visible from almost everywhere on Eigg,
the improbable Sgurr adds an element of
surrealist drama to the landscape. Its
alien appearance suggests it was beamed
in from outer space, but the truth is
almost as incredible. Some 60 million
years ago, the Isle of Rum volcano
erupted, forming Eigg and its
neighbouring islands. Further eruptions
filled a winding riverbed with molten lava
which then cooled to form pitchstone.
This proved to be much harder than the
surrounding rocks which over time
eroded leaving an inversion of the
original landform, looking quite as if it
had just been released from a jelly mould.

Start from the shop and café near the
pier at Galmisdale Bay, the island hub,
although most of the population live in
the north of the island. Follow the road
uphill to the left of the standing stone (it
is, in fact, a basalt column originally from
the Sgurr itself) which was erected to
commemorate the purchase of the island
by the local community in partnership
with Highland Council and the Scottish

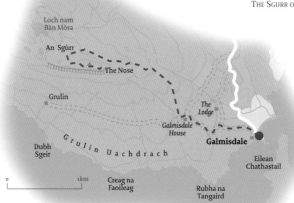

Wildlife Trust in 1997. The buyout has been a catalyst for a number of community projects and enterprises, including a renewal energy scheme, accommodation for visitors and a firewood company.

Pass the entrance to the Lodge and the green community hall off to the right and keep climbing uphill. At the gate go through the field, aiming for the house at Galmisdale with An Sgurr looming beyond. Stay on the track which skirts to the right of the house and go through the gate, then turn left onto another track which leads to the abandoned settlement of Grulin. However, the route for An Sgurr turns off to the right just past the house – look out for the path marked with a small cairn and red waymarker.

This winds uphill over heather and bracken, aiming directly for the prow of An Sgurr which stands at the far end of a mile-long lava-flow ridge. Sometimes boggy underfoot, the path then coils

round the north side of this volcanic lump, with views to a number of small moorland lochans with the Isle of Rum far beyond. About one-third of the way along the base of An Sgurr the path starts rising uphill to climb a distinct cleft in the rock. This tops out on a wide shoulder of knobbly, rocky ground. The route heads over to the far side of the shoulder where, delineated by occasional red-paint markers, a small but clear path picks its way around and up the rocky ridge. Several undulations follow, before eventually gaining the circular trig point at the 393m-high summit.

From here spectacular views can be enjoyed in all directions. On a clear day, all the Small Isles can be seen, as well as the peaks on the mainland and the Cuillin on Skye. Take extreme care – there are vertical drops all around. To return to Galmisdale you need to retrace your outward route.

Massacre and Cathedral Caves

Distance 3.6km Time 2 hours
Terrain track and grassy path, steep
narrow paths to caves; Cathedral Cave
only accessible at low tide – torch needed
for Massacre Cave Map OS Explorer 397
Access ferry to Eigg pier from Mallaig,
limited summer service from Arisaig

Combine the majesty of nature with
a gruesome human history on this
exploration of two large sea caves.
The massive Cathedral Cave can only be
entered at low tide, and a scramble over
slippery pebbles and rocks is needed to
reach it. A torch is required to venture
into the depths of Massacre Cave.
The possibility of rockfall makes these
caves dangerous places to explore
– take extreme care and do not advance
if there is evidence of recent rockfall.

From the pier and shop building head
straight up the road, passing to the left of
the standing stone and continuing past
the entrance to the Lodge and community

hall. Immediately after passing this green
building on your right, take the track on
the left. The route is marked occasionally
with purple waypoints. Carry on until the
route approaches a house, then bear left
to drop slightly downhill.

The grassy path offers good views of
Eilean Chathastail and its small
lighthouse. Further afield you may be
able to make out the Treshnish Isles and
the prominent shape of the Dutchman's
Cap beyond the Isle of Muck. Keep right
when the path forks, staying just above a
group of stones and aiming for a gate in
the fence ahead.

After passing through the gate, cross
the field to another gate leading to a
narrow path down the cliff. Walk down
some steps and cross a small bridge over a
burn; you then need to choose which cave
to explore first – this will be largely
dependent on the state of the tide – the
Cathedral Cave is along the coast to the
right and the Massacre Cave to the left.

◀ Cathedral Cave

The Cathedral Cave can only be entered at low tide and you need to leave enough time to get back round a small rocky section of coast that is normally underwater. To head for this cave keep on the path ahead which narrows and then ends on the rocky shoreline. Take care as you cross the slippery tidal rocks, rounding the base of a cliff to reach the massive entrance to the cave. It was used to host Catholic masses during the persecution after 1746 and later by Free Church dissenters.

To visit the Massacre Cave return to the point where the path splits and this time walk down a steep path which then rears up to reach the small cave entrance. A continual drip of water over the entrance usually sends visitors hurrying into the cave proper. After an initial squeeze this opens out dramatically.

The 80m-long cave was the scene of one of the most ruthless acts in a clan feud in the late 14th century. Seeking revenge for an earlier atrocity by Clan MacDonald, a group of MacLeods from Skye landed on

Eigg and spent a couple of days searching for the residents who, having seen the boat arriving, had hidden in this cave. When the MacLeods were sailing away on the third day they spotted a lookout from the cave; the boat quickly turned around and by following footprints the Skyemen were able to locate the hiding place. Blocking the entrance they lit a fire trapping and killing 395 Eigachs. Human bones have been discovered in a number of excavations over the years. Later, the MacDonalds exacted bloody revenge by killing a similar number of MacLeods at Trumpan Church on Skye.

Emerging into the peaceful daylight of modern-day Eigg, the return is back up the cliff and along the outward route to the pier.

The Lodge

Galmisdale

Uamh Chràbhaichd
cave

Uamh Fhraing
caves

A' Chleit

Eilean Chathastail

0   500m

Rubha na Tangaird

The Finger of God

Distance 5.75km **Time** 3 hours
Terrain steep hill path, some navigation
needed; return route crosses some boggy
ground **Map** OS Explorer 397
Access no public transport to the start,
which is just over 5km from the ferry
pier. Ferry to Eigg pier from Mallaig,
limited summer service from Arisaig

**This divine walk climbs above the cliffs
behind Cleadale, passing a rock pinnacle
known as the Finger of God. The route
follows an escarpment with sweeping
views over sandy beaches to the
mountains of Rum and Skye, and can be
combined with visits to the Singing
Sands and Laig Beach for a full day out.**

Start from Cleadale, the main
settlement at the north end of Eigg where
many visitors choose to stay. The road
from the ferry pier leads here, taking

about an hour on foot; alternatively you
can hire bikes at the pier or arrange a taxi
ride. The walk begins from the fork in the
road at the south end of Cleadale where
the war memorial sits on a small outcrop.
This spot was traditionally the island's
'parliament' where the men would
discuss upcoming jobs and the trials and
tribulations of island life, presumably
while the womenfolk actually got on with
the work! From this point Bidean an
Tigherna, the Finger of God, points
skyward from the top of the escarpment.

With the war memorial behind you, take
the road south (back towards the ferry
pier) for a short distance before turning
up a grassy path just beyond Lageorna
B&B. This rises steeply uphill, taking you
over a stile and towards a gully which you
enter for a steepening climb. Relief is
provided when you meet a narrow path

Dùnan
Thalasgair

Blàr Mòr

Coire
na Falain

Camas
Sgiotaig

B e i n n   B h u i d h e

Sgorr an
Fharaidh

traversing the base
of the cliffs; bear
right (south) along
this. It soon zigzags up the
less steep gully to the right,
passing the remains of an
old drystane dyke before
topping out on the heather
moorland to the southwest
of the Finger of God.

Turn left to follow the
edge of the dramatic
escarpment with views
down to the fertile
croftland of Cleadale,
the white sandy beaches and
on a clear day over to the
mountains of Rum. Ravens can often
be seen circling the Finger of God which
stands proud of the main ridge.

A rough path continues along the cliff
edge. It is wet underfoot in a couple of
places and crosses a small burn before
eventually reaching the high point of
Sgorr an Fharaidh. From here it's possible
to pick out the individual mountains of
Skye's Cuillin range. It's a great spot to
soak up a view that takes in most of Eigg,
with often only a sheep or raven or two
for company.

Carry on along the escarpment, passing
to the left of the trig point which is
actually a little lower than the unmarked
summit of Sgorr an Fharaidh. The route
continues towards the steep-sided Dunan
Thalasgair. Follow a fence (on your left)

Bay of
Laig

Cleadale

To
Galmisdale

A' Chuagach

Bidean an
Tighearna

0   1km

before passing through a gate. Instead of
following the more obvious path onto the
rocky knobble to the right, aim west along
the faint path that drops downhill. This
soon becomes clearer as it descends
steeply in a series of zigzags.

Keep to the left of a fence; when the
ruined buildings at Howlin are clearly
visible, aim left towards them on an
indistinct and sometimes boggy path.
Stay well below the modern house on the
left to eventually reach the ruin and stone
barn. Take the sometimes muddy track
behind them to pass below a white croft
house. This soon becomes a surfaced road
which leads through Cleadale to the start.

◀ Looking towards Rum from the Finger of God

Singing Sands from Cleadale

Distance 3.7km **Time** 1 hour 30
Terrain minor road, boggy path through grazing land (dogs to be kept under strict control) **Map** OS Explorer 397
Access no public transport to the start, which is just over 5km from the ferry pier. Ferry to Eigg pier from Mallaig, limited summer service from Arisaig

Possibly the loveliest of Eigg's beaches (although competition is fierce), this short ramble should leave plenty of time to see if you can make the sands 'sing' whilst gazing over the sea to the Rum Cuillin.

This walk starts from Cleadale where there are a number of accommodation options. If coming from Galmisdale you can either make the 5km approach route on foot or by bike (bike hire near the pier), or combine this with the rougher moorland and forestry walk to Laig.

Begin by the war memorial cairn at the fork in the road at the southern end of Cleadale. Facing the memorial, take the left branch to head slightly downhill. Cleadale is the most concentrated settlement on Eigg, a scattering of houses and fertile croftland sheltered below formidable high cliffs and overseen by the rock pinnacle known as the Finger of God. Looking out across the sea to the Isle of Rum, the setting couldn't be more dramatic.

Where the surfaced road ends near a bungalow to the left, carry straight on along a rough track, passing through a gate. Keep an eye out for the occasional blue markers on stones and posts as the route bears left and then steers to the right of a sheep fank, aiming for the coast. Over to the left, the Bay of Laig is overshadowed by the prominent ridge of the Sgurr of Eigg, a curious feature formed as a result of a volcanic eruption on Rum.

The faint path soon bears right to cross

◄ Driftwood on the Singing Sands

open grazing land, aiming for a gap in the remains of a drystane dyke. After a short while Camas Sgiotaig, the Bay of the Singing Sands, comes into view ahead. Either cross a stile over the fence, or continue to the right to pass through a gate, although this route is sometimes muddy. The path soon descends towards the beach, zigzagging on its way down and crossing another stile to access the beach itself.

Here, the sand consists of pure quartz grains ground from the Jurassic rocks at this end of the island by the sea. If dry the grains squeak as you scuff your feet in walking across the beach; to call this singing may be a stretch, but it is still an eerie sound. The grains are from rocks formed over 145 million years ago – when this area was a lagoon populated by sea turtles, crocodiles and plesiosaurs.

Driftwood on the beach often comes with its own colony of goose barnacles. These large mussel-like crustaceans were once thought to develop into barnacle geese. No-one had even seen barnacle geese breed – migration was unknown at that time. As the barnacles were usually found on driftwood and were the same colour as the geese, it was thought they were effectively goose eggs which had been laid on a branch of a tree and later fallen into the sea.

At low tide it is possible to explore beyond the high wave-cut overhang on the left and head up a pebble-strewn rock gash and through a rock arch to reach another beach. At very low tides you can scramble and beachcomb all the way along the coast back to Laig Bay; however, this route returns inland.

Leave the beach and head back up the cliff path towards the gate and along the fence to the stile. Climb this and aim directly inland on a faint path with some marker posts. After the path bears right it reaches double gates; go through one of these and head towards the white house at Howlin. Keeping the fence on your right go through a gate in the stone wall to meet a track. Turn right along the track to reach the road, then bear right to return to the start.

Rum is the largest of the Small Isles, its jagged Cuillin Ridge a familiar sight from its neighbours. The wild interior of the island is reflected in its reputation for challenging hillwalks, but even though it is a mecca for climbers and mountaineers there are still plenty of easier walks to occupy a couple of days. Inhabited since Neolithic times, Rum was cleared of its remaining indigenous population in the late 18th century to make way for sheep and later deer as the island became a private sporting estate for the wealthy. The most notable owner was George Bullough, the millionaire son of a textile industrialist who spent the summer stalking deer on the island; he built the fantastic and incongruous Kinloch Castle. The island's isolation continued when ownership passed to the state and Rum was given over to conservation and a long-term study of the red deer. Whilst most of the island remains in the hands of Scottish Natural Heritage, the area around Kinloch is now community owned and a number of initiatives are seeking to improve the infrastructure and provide a sustainable future for residents.

The Bullough Mausoleum ▶

Rum

Northside Nature Trail

Distance 5.5km Time 2 hours
Terrain easy tracks and waymarked
paths Map OS Explorer 397 Access ferry
from Mallaig, limited summer service
from Arisaig

This walk is ideal if you only have a short
time on Rum between boats. It gives you
the chance to visit the castle and offers
an introduction to the island, taking in
the croftland of the Kinloch Glen and the
coast of Loch Scresort.

From the ferry jetty take the track
towards Rum's main settlement, Kinloch.
The route passes the primary school and
then keeps right through trees to pass the
old pier. Follow the signed track past the
bunkhouse and the island's shoreside
camping area. At the next junction carry
straight on for Kinloch Castle, soon
arriving at the massive red sandstone
stately home.

Tours of the castle are timed to coincide
with the ferry on days when it is possible
to make a day visit to Rum – check at the
castle entrance for the time. Stepping
through the doors you get a taste of the
extravagance and eccentricity of George
Bullough who built it as a holiday
shooting lodge in the late 1890s following
his father's purchase of the island. George
and his French wife, Monica, travelled
extensively, often in a palatial oceangoing
racing yacht which they moored in Loch
Scresort during the summers they spent
on Rum. The Bulloughs made their
money in the textile machinery industry
and at one time ranked in the top 10 of
the world's wealthiest people. The castle,
although now in a perilous state of decay,
contains many objects from the
Bulloughs' travels, as well as innovations
such as electricity and en suite facilities
with showers and flushing toilets –
cutting edge at the time.

Continue past the castle and go straight

◀ Kinloch Castle

on at a crossroads to cross a bridge. The island's shop and café are just a short detour here, but our route turns immediately left after the bridge onto a track with yellow eagle waymarkers. Almost straight away turn right through a gate onto a grassy path running uphill by the edge of a wood. At the top of the rise pass through a gateway in a stone wall and aim left through the trees which provide a welcome habitat for many birds, including warblers.

Pass the Millionth Tree, planted in 1997 to commemorate the island's 40 years as a National Nature Reserve, a designation it received on being sold to the nation after Monica's death. Most of the island is now managed by Scottish Natural Heritage and, although it gained a reputation as the 'Forbidden Isle' as early access was very restricted, this was gradually relaxed. The Land Reform Act formalised access rights, and the local community has now purchased the area around Kinloch and started a number of initiatives aimed at making life on Rum more sustainable.

The path traverses the slope above open croftland. This is a good area to look out for hen harriers and eagles, as well as groundnesting birds; in the distance across the glen are the peaks of Hallival and Barkeval. The path passes above Croft 3, one of a number of crofts established following the community buyout. Rum was once a well populated island, supporting around 400 people at its peak in the 1790s. The decline in the kelp industry began the tide of departures from Rum, but this was compounded by the island being leased to Lachlan Maclean for sheep farming; by 1828 it is estimated that all the original tenants had been cleared and shepherds were brought in from nearby Skye and Muck.

Follow a yellow marker to begin heading downhill beside a burn. At the bottom, curve left along the Kinloch River to soon pass a shed selling croft produce and crafts. Continuing on the path, you eventually cross a footbridge, keeping left when you meet the main track. This soon leads to the crossroads near Kinloch Castle – go straight on to reach the loch shore, passing a house and phonebox, with a good view of the castle. Turn left at the next junction to return past the bunkhouse and campsite to the jetty.

Port na Caranean and the otter hide

Distance 2.5km (1km to otter hide and back) Time 2 hours (1 hour for otter hide only) Terrain good path to otter hide, rough, boggy, overgrown in places and navigation skills needed for onward route Map OS Explorer 397 Access ferry from Mallaig, limited summer service from Arisaig

A short woodland path from the pier leads to a turf-roofed coastal hide from which to search for otters, seals and seabirds. The optional extension covers much rougher ground above the waterside to reach the deserted ruins of Port na Caranean – a delightful and tranquil spot to explore.

Start from the Calmac ferry pier, walking up past the waiting room and boat shed. Once on the track, look out for the path on the left waymarked with an otter symbol. Take this, soon passing

some seats and a stone memorial to the author, environmentalist and hillwalker Irvine Butterfield. As well as founding Mountaineering Scotland and contributing to other Scottish outdoors organisations, Butterfield was involved in the restoration of the bothy at Dibidil further round the coast from here. The inscription on the back of the stone is from William Blake: 'Great things are done when men and mountains meet; This is not done by jostling in the street'.

The path soon dives into the woods where a number of ruined houses can still be made out on both sides. Rum's population peaked at around 400 in the 1790s when it was ruled by Clan Maclean. Somewhat dependent on the kelp industry, the island economy suffered when the price of kelp plummeted as other cheaper substitutes were developed. The island was leased to a Maclean

◄ The otter hide

relative who cleared the remaining inhabitants to make way for sheep, whilst a later owner introduced red deer to provide a sporting estate lifestyle alongside the sheep. It is thought that none of the original Rum residents remained after 1828, with new shepherds brought in from Skye and Muck.

Where the path forks, keep left to find the beautifully constructed otter hide. Here you can view records of recent sightings and spend some time looking out for the telltale V-shaped ripple in the water that signals a swimming otter.

From this point, the walk to Port na Caranean becomes much rougher and wetter and the path hard to follow –

anyone just wanting an easy ramble should retrace steps from the hide. Otherwise continue on a faint path at the edge of the trees above the pebbly shore. The path is faint and very boggy for this first section, but soon becomes clearer as you emerge from the trees and cross heather moorland above the sea.

Eventually the remains of a coppiced woodland signal the start of the deserted township of Port na Caranean. The five houses here are thought to have been built for crofters from Skye who, having been evicted themselves during the Clearances, were brought to Rum to help manage the sheep; they lived here for around 30 years before being moved to Kinloch in 1861. Today it is a beautiful place with stunning views across the water to Skye and the mainland.

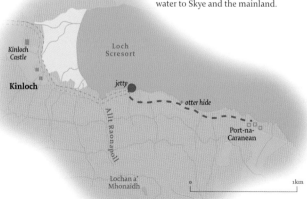

Kilmory Bay

Distance 18.5km Time 6 hours (round trip) Terrain Landrover tracks suitable for mountain bikes, short boggy path to beach Map OS Explorer 397 Access ferry from Mallaig, limited summer service from Arisaig

Once a forbidden place as a result of the long-term study into red deer being carried out there, Kilmory Bay retains a magical feeling of otherworldliness. The stunning sandy beach looks directly across to the Skye Cuillin and is accessed by a long but easy walk on a track; it is also a great route for mountain bikers.

Starting from the Calmac ferry pier, head along the track leading to the main settlement of Kinloch along the shores of Loch Scresort. Fork right after the tiny primary school to soon reach the old pier, then keep left round the shore track to pass the island's camping area and,

shortly after, the bunkhouse. At the next junction carry on ahead for Kinloch Castle to soon pass the front of the impressive red sandstone pile built as a holiday shooting lodge for George Bullough whose father had bought the island in 1879. Although currently in a decaying state, no expense was spared on its construction and furnishing in 1897 and it is well worth fitting in a tour to see the grand excesses of the interior and hear some of the extravagant stories about the eccentric owners.

After the castle turn left at a crossroads and follow the track as it climbs alongside the Kinloch River. Stony at first, the surface improves once the gradient levels out. The route leaves the trees and passes through a gate; watch out for an impressive waterfall on the left. After about 3km the track forks – the left branch continues uphill before finally

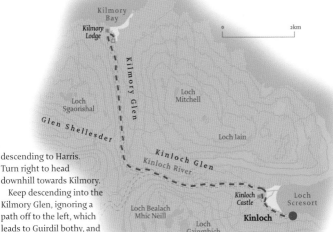

0   2km

Kilmory Bay

Kilmory Lodge

Kilmory Glen

Loch Mitchell

Loch Sgaorishal

Glen Shellesder

Loch Iain

Kinloch Glen
Kinloch River

Loch Bealach Mhic Neill

Loch Gainmhich

Kinloch Castle

Loch Scresort

Kinloch

descending to Harris. Turn right to head downhill towards Kilmory.

Keep descending into the Kilmory Glen, ignoring a path off to the left, which leads to Guirdil bothy, and passing a couple of fenced woodlands. The whole of Rum is a National Nature Reserve, but since 1972 this part of the island has hosted a detailed study into the behaviour of red deer by Edinburgh and Cambridge Universities. The red deer stags on Rum tend to be a little larger than their mainland counterparts which is attributed in part to the amount of nutrient-rich seaweed which supplements their diet. The herd has also starred in the BBC's *Autumnwatch* TV series which recorded the daily battles between the alpha males during the rutting season.

Keep on the main track, ignoring a small branch off to the right and eventually nearing one of the cottages used by the researchers. Respect the privacy of the occupants and keep away from the cottage, instead leaving the track at a boulder with 'beach' faintly painted on it.

From here the going is boggy and rough; stay on the right-hand edge of a rocky knoll. Soon you gain your reward – the stunning sandy beach of Kilmory Bay with views seaward to the peaks of the Skye Cuillin. The more adventurous can venture further east to visit more beaches and the remains of summer shielings, but the going is very rough and navigation skills and a map are needed. Most visitors are content to relax on the beach or watch the deer.

Before returning it is worth detouring a short distance upstream along the burn to reach an old burial ground where it is usually easy to spot groups of deer. Take care not to disturb them and keep any dogs under very close control. Return back along the path and then climb the track up Kilmory Glen to retrace the outward route back to Kinloch.

◀ Looking over Kilmory Bay to the Cuillin of Skye

Barkeval and Hallival

Distance 13.5km **Time** 7 hours
Terrain good footpath into the coire, then
pathless, rough and rocky going with
some easy scrambling **Map** OS Explorer
397 **Access** ferry from Mallaig, limited
summer service from Arisaig

Rum is dominated by its fearsome Cuillin
Ridge – smaller twin to the more famous
Cuillin on Skye. The full traverse is one of
Scotland's toughest outings – an epic day
with hard scrambling – but this more
modest ascent of two outlying peaks
gives a taste of this dramatic mountain
environment. It still makes for a
challenging steep and rocky hillwalk
requiring care and navigation skills.
A shorter version would be to just walk
up into the corrie, a fine walk in itself.

Start from the ferry pier and head along
the track towards Kinloch, forking right
after the primary school to pass the old
pier and then following the track past the
campsite and bunkhouse. Carry straight

on when signed for the castle, but
immediately before it turn left onto
a red-waymarked track for Coire Dubh.
A gate on the left gives access to a path
that winds through the trees by the burn,
soon passing the old hydro building. Built
as George Bullough's island holiday home
in 1897, Kinloch Castle was the first private
residence in Scotland to have electricity,
powered from a dam in Coire Dubh. The
island is still largely powered by hydro;
the new building sits behind the old
stone one.

At a gateway, turn left along a wider
path, soon passing a National Nature
Reserve sign. The route gradually climbs
out of the trees onto open moorland,
crossing small burns and staying close to
the Allt Slugan a' Choilich with its pools
and small waterfalls. When the constructed
path ends at a modern dam, a rougher
path takes over, initially rising close to the
burn, then aiming right to pass between
tall gateposts before returning to the burn.

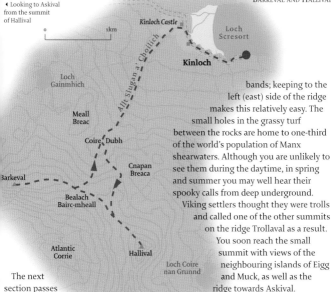

◀ Looking to Askival from the summit of Hallival

Kinloch Castle

Loch Scresort

Kinloch

Loch Gainmhich

Meall Breac

Coire Dubh

Cnapan Breaca

Barkeval

Bealach Bairc-mheall

Atlantic Corrie

Hallival

Loch Coire nan Grunnd

Askival

0   1km

bands; keeping to the left (east) side of the ridge makes this relatively easy. The small holes in the grassy turf between the rocks are home to one-third of the world's population of Manx shearwaters. Although you are unlikely to see them during the daytime, in spring and summer you may well hear their spooky calls from deep underground.

Viking settlers thought they were trolls and called one of the other summits on the ridge Trollaval as a result. You soon reach the small summit with views of the neighbouring islands of Eigg and Muck, as well as the ridge towards Askival.

Follow the ridge back down but continue beyond the point you joined it to reach the Bealach Bairc-mheall. From here the gentler climb to the top of Barkeval begins, passing a cairn and then a massive rocky outcrop before the broad rock-strewn ridge leads to the true summit of Barkeval at a cairn at 591m. There are great views across to the hills on Rum, as well as down to Harris Bay and the Bullough Mausoleum.

Return to the Bealach Bairc-mheall; from the lowest point a faint and initially steep path descends into Coire Dubh, adjacent to a small burn. Rejoin the outward route at the old dam and retrace your steps to Kinloch.

The next section passes above an impressive deep box canyon carved through the rock by the burn. When you reach the remains of the old stone dam, cross this and, after climbing the grassy slope ahead, a clearer path takes you southeast up to Cnapan Breaca. The gradient eases off and though pathless a route aiming SSW will avoid any rocky difficulties; it is just a steep and rocky slog to gain the ridge. There is a great view of the Rum Cuillin peaks with the highest mountain, Askival, prominent in the foreground. Keep heading towards Hallival along the broad ridge.

As you gain height, you need to pick your way through a number of rocky

Orval and Harris odyssey

Distance 27km **Time** 8 hours 30
Terrain track, boggy moorland, pathless
at times; a mountain bike could be used
for the approach **Map** OS Explorer 397
Access ferry from Mallaig, limited
summer service from Arisaig

This long hillwalk explores the wild and
craggy heart of the island, climbing to
the fantastic summit viewpoint of Orval,
before descending to Harris where the
Bulloughs' impressive mausoleum
overlooks the sea. The section over the
hills is pathless and good navigation
skills are essential; a mountain bike
would reduce the amount of track
walking at the start and finish.

   Start from Rum's ferry pier and follow
the track along the coastline to Kinloch,
following the signs for the bunkhouse
and then the castle. After passing in front
of this stately and ever so slightly bizarre

pile, take the next left at the crossroads.
As this track climbs alongside the Kinloch
River, it is at times steep and stony but
soon improves underfoot as the gradient
eases. Pass through a gate and when the
track forks after 3km take the upper track
on the left to continue to Malcolm's
Bridge, the second bridge after the fork.
This is where you should leave your bike
if cycling. Do not cross the bridge but turn
right onto a grassy trail running next to a
burn. Originally the route to the mines on
Bloodstone Hill, the path has become
faint and boggy in places but with care
can be followed across the moorland on a
wide loop to climb to the Bealach a'
Bhraigh Bhig.

   From this shoulder, leave the path and
aim southwest towards Orval, keeping
well to the left on the initial climb. Once
above this steep section, carry on along
the top of the sheer cliffs with sweeping

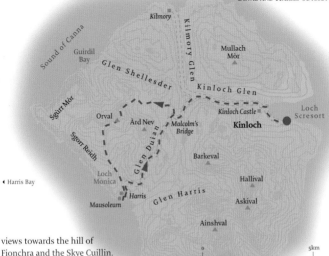

◀ Harris Bay

views towards the hill of
Fionchra and the Skye Cuillin.
Cross the plateau in a southerly
direction and then curve round to
aim for Orval's summit which
is marked with a trig point and cairn.
This is a great spot to enjoy the views
over much of Rum and to the island of
Canna to the north.

Continue in the same direction,
descending to a small bealach. From this,
bear south over the minor top marked on
the map at 520m. The long, rough and
pathless descent aims initially for Loch
Monica but then swings further left (east)
to avoid the rougher ground and to drop
closer to the Glen Duian River. As the
whitewashed Harris Lodge comes into
view, head towards this and then the
imposing mausoleum beyond, eventually
joining the track for the last section.

Built in the style of a Doric temple, this
is the final resting place of the Bullough
family. The three outsize slabs mark the
graves of George Bullough who built
Kinloch Castle, his wife Monica and his
father John. From the mausoleum you can
detour east down to a small sandy beach
where wild goats often forage for
seaweed. The return route is a long one,
following the Landrover track climbing
uphill from Harris, but the route is often
enlivened by encounters with Rum
ponies, as well as clusters of red deer and
sometimes more goats. If you've left a
mountain bike at Malcolm's Bridge you'll
be glad of it for the last stretch downhill
to Kinloch.

Muck is a little green goddess – the smallest of the Small Isles at less than 4km by 2km, its fertile farmland, sandy beaches and beautiful coastline provide a complete retreat from mainstream tourism. Less visited than the other islands and with a population of less than 40, if you stay for more than a day you start to feel like part of the community here.

The island has a number of superb walks, including the sands at Gallanach overlooking the distinct rugged profile of Rum; you can easily absorb half a day beachcombing as you relax into 'island time'. Muck is home to corncrakes, so listen out for their distinctive 'craking' sound as they eye you from the flag iris and nettles. The complete circuit of the island is a rewarding undertaking, requiring an overnight stay – there is a wide variety of accommodation for such a small island, including a bunkhouse at the community hall, a fine new lodge, self-catering, bed & breakfast and a seasonal yurt. There is also a café – booking required in the evenings – showcasing the best of the food produced on the island.

Muck sunset ▶

Muck

Caisteal an Duin Bhain

Distance 3.25km Time 1 hour
Terrain track, pathless, rough grazing
land Map OS Explorer 397
Access Calmac ferry from Mallaig

This short walk from the ferry pier at Port Mor follows a beautiful section of pathless coastline to visit the site of a medieval fort.

Start from the jetty where the ferry arrives near Port Mor, Muck's main settlement. Follow the track leading past the houses, old pier, shop and café. Keep heading along the road until you encounter a junction and turn left here. This passes beneath the remains of a chapel and the island cemetery.

Muck's population peaked at 144 in the 18th century, but with around 40 residents today its numbers are stable compared to some other islands of similar size. As Gaelic speakers have left, Muck has managed to attract new blood to replace them, with families moving in from all around the UK. The island consists of a single farm with around 50 cattle and 450 sheep. It takes in most of the land and its houses, and has been owned and run by the MacEwen family – themselves resident on the island – since early in the 20th century.

At a fork in the track branch right to climb uphill, bending right to pass a stone-built house. Keep climbing and at

the bend before the track reaches
a house at the top of the hill, leave
the track to bear left (southeast)
along the open grassy ridge.

Continue along the left edge of the
ridge – it can be rough underfoot in
places – before it eventually descends
towards the distinctive outcrop of
Caisteal an Duin Bhàin. The flat-topped
dome is in a strategic position with a
great outlook. Some sections of
stonework can be seen; rectangular
structures inside are thought to be
medieval, constructed on the site of a
much earlier fort or dun. From here the
return route is to retrace your steps back
along the ridge and down to Port Mor.

Port Mor ▼

41

Aird nan Uan

**Distance 6.75km Time 2 hours 30
Terrain minor road and track, rough path
Map OS Explorer 397 Access Calmac ferry
from Mallaig**

**Cross the Isle of Muck using its tiny main
road to reach the fine sandy beaches at
Gallanach. Here you can soak up the
superb views over to Rum and check out
the ancient burial site at Aird nan Uan.**

From the ferry jetty take the road to the
left which soon leads through Port Mor,
where most of the population of Muck
live. Pass the small gift shop and excellent
café, and stay on the main road.

The route crosses the fertile little island
to soon reach the north side which boasts
grandstand views towards the mountains
on Rum. After the road reaches the north
coast continue past the new Gallanach
Lodge and then Gallanach Farm. Since the
new pier was built in 2005 livestock can be
taken to the mainland and on to market
by the vehicle ferry – previously they
faced a complicated and potentially
perilous journey by small launch.

On this section, the route passes the
stunning sandy beaches of Gallanach –
well worth exploring if you have time.
Otherwise continue along the road and

through a gate to reach the road end at some farm buildings. Aim right onto a path leading behind the corrugated shed and towards a house up above the coast. Just before you reach the house, bear left over a stile and make your way uphill to gain the grassy ridge above.

The ridge runs NNW, aiming directly for the outlying islands of Eilean Aird nan Uan (Sheep island) and the larger Eilean nan Each (Horse Island). The former can be reached by a short scramble but the latter is inaccessible except for a very brief time at the lowest of tides. Many birds nest on Horse Island, including Muck's only colony of puffins. Before the islands you come to a ring of stones – this is the remains of a Bronze Age chambered cairn, with three much more recent graves added to it. It is a fabulous spot to sit and take in the views over the islands.

From the cairn the return is by the outward route, though it's hard to resist a stop-off at the beach and at the island café along the way.

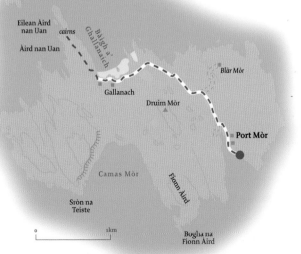

◀ Boat at Gallanach Bay

Beinn Airein by Gallanach Bay

Distance 7km Time 3 hours
Terrain **minor road, path and pathless moorland requiring navigation skills and map; dogs to be kept under tight control**
Map **OS Explorer 397** Access **Calmac ferry from Mallaig**

Pass beautiful Gallanach Beach before making your ascent of the highest summit on Muck, with views over the whole island.

From the ferry jetty turn left along the track and pass through the small settlement of Port Mor. Carry on along the road, ignoring the turning to the left and following this to the north side of the island where there are amazing views across to the mountainous Isle of Rum. The route passes the bright white sandy beaches of Gallanach which deserve a detour if time and weather allows. Pass the farm buildings on the shoreside and, after the last building on the left, turn left opposite the path to Gallanach Cottage and go through a small metal gate before rising gently uphill.

Bear slightly right as you make your ascent and then left, aiming south towards Beinn Airein which is prominent ahead. Keep making for the corner of a field and pass through the gate ahead into an area planted with native trees. Carry straight on initially, before bearing slightly right to follow a faint grassy track. Pass through another farm gate as the route continues to rise. Keep the fence on your right and eventually a gap in this leads to much rougher ground. The climb continues until you gain the summit of Beinn Airein, marked with a cylindrical trig point; it's a stunning viewpoint.

From here, it is possible to simply

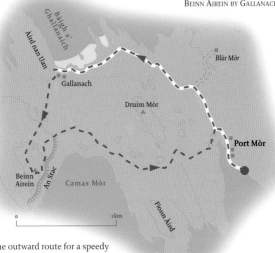

retrace the outward route for a speedy return to Port Mor. However, this shorter but much rougher crosscountry return adds to the challenge – mapreading skills are essential. From the summit aim east downhill, following a sheep trod through a break in the crags to reach the grassy terrain below where a gap in a fence leads into the next field. Keep heading downhill to a small gate in the next fence which brings you onto the grassy area behind the bay of Camas Mor – this makes a great detour if you have time. Otherwise stay away from the shore and follow the fence east across level ground, crossing a drainage ditch at one point.

Climb the steep ground on the far side of the bay to later pass a patch of woodland to the left and reach a stone sheep fank. To the right is a gate in the drystane dyke; go through this and bear diagonally right across the field, aiming

for the southern end of a small lochan. From here continue in the same direction and go through a gate at the field corner. Head uphill, bearing left on a faint track; at a fork, branch right towards the coast and go through a farm gate. Beyond this, turn left and keep the fence on your left as you bear due east.

Carry on ahead to cross the small glen with the ruined settlement and trees near the sea (in very wet conditions this boggy area can be avoided by following an inland path). Bear left at a ruined drystane dyke and keep heading east. A house comes into range with a view to the Isle of Eigg beyond. From this point descend to a track and turn right along it, swinging right at the road to pass the café at Port Mor and return to the start.

◀ The fertile fields of Muck

Coastal round of Muck

Distance 14km Time 6 hours
Terrain pathless grazing land and
moorland, navigation skills and map
needed, keep dogs under tight control
Map OS Explorer 397 Access Calmac ferry
from Mallaig

Challenge yourself to walk around the
entire island, taking in moorland,
farmland, cliffs and beaches with a chance
to spot wildlife and meet the locals.

Start by turning left from the slipway to
follow the track into Port Mor. Follow the
sign on the right for the café and once
past the stone building take the track
heading uphill behind it, going through a
gate below the community hall. The track
swings left through a second gate and
continues to rise, passing a house to reach
the open moor. Leave the track where it
turns sharp right towards a building and
instead aim east to pass the ruins of an
old house at Carndearg. Head towards the
coast but stay on the grassy clifftops to

bear north rather than dropping down to
the shore.

There are great views from these low
cliffs which include a couple of caves.
At a fence bear left for a short distance to
reach a fence before aiming for Am Maol,
the northeasterly headland of Muck which
has a great view across to Rum. Keep
heading round the coast, passing through
a gate in the next fence and then keeping
on the grassy shoreline to the right of
another fence. After this fence take a path
leading inland towards a bungalow,
eventually reaching the road. Turn right
and soon the road shadows the coastline
and passes the sandy beaches and farm
at Gallanach.

Go through a gate to the end of the road
and turn right onto a path here, passing
behind a corrugated iron building. Just
before a house is reached take the stile on
the left and head along the crest of the
grassy ridge – the Aird nan Uan. Near the
far end are the remains of a Bronze Age

Eilean
nan Each

Eilean Àird
nan Uan

Bàgh
a' Ghallanaich

Àird nan Uan

Am Maol

Blar Mor

Gallanach

Rubh' Leam
na Làraich

◄ Rum and Eigg from
the Muck coast

Beinn
Airein

Port Mòr

Camas Mòr

Sròn na Teiste

Caisteal an
Duin Bhain

cairn with several more modern graves alongside it. Turns south to pass around the back of an inlet where the ground can be boggy at times, aiming for the little turf-roofed cottage at the head of the inlet. Pass in front of this and continue above the shore until you come to a break in the crags on the left. Head through this and follow the rough sheep trods high above the coast.

To reach the cliffs on the west side of the island bear west across open country, aiming just left of some crags to climb a grassy brae from where you can detour to the highest point on this section of cliff to take in the great views. Otherwise continue on the springy turf; eventually the route aims eastwards. After undulating over several humps it reaches the bottom of the climb up Beinn Airein which follows a small path heading diagonally to the left at first before turning right for the final pull.

The flat summit, topped by a trig point, is a wonderful viewpoint. From here head east downhill, aiming for a gap in the fence. Cross the field to reach a gate in the next fence which opens on to the grassy area at the back of Camas Mor. From here continue east to a gate in a drystone wall and then bear diagonally right through the next field to a gate in the corner. Now take the track to head southeast before soon turning right to rejoin the coast. At a final fence, detour inland to reach a gate and then keep to the high ground above the cliffs, aiming for the rocky mound of Caisteal an Duin Bhain which was once topped with a medieval fort.

Take the path leading north, staying well above the sea. At a fork stay on the higher left branch to continue along the top of the grassy ridge. Turn right at a track to head down past a stone house, soon reaching another track. Turn left here and at the road turn right, passing the café to return to the start.

Hidden from the mainland by the rugged profile of Rum, it's easy to overlook Canna. With a stunning coastline, a fascinating history of human habitation right up to the present day and plenty of wildlife – including a large colony of puffins on a spectacular sea stack – it's well worth the extra time at sea to reach it.

Canna

A'Chill

Sanday

Sound of Canna

So

Rum

Loch S

Kinloch

The island is popular with visiting yachts which moor in the sheltered bay where the ferry docks. From here a gentle ramble explores two fascinating churches, Canna House, the former home of folklorist and Gaelic scholar John Lorne Campbell, its lush gardens providing a surprising and restful retreat and then on to an almost inaccessible castle perched on a high coastal crag.

Further from the main settlement the walks explore fertile pastures, small woodlands, wild moorland and dramatic cliffs. An ancient carved cross and two Iron Age souterrains provide fascinating evidence of early habitation and you can also try out the punishment stone where local law-breakers were forced to sit with their thumb jammed in a hole in the stone at the mercy of the elements and midges! The challenging coastal circuit provides a wild expedition with fabulous views of Rum, the Skye Cuillin and the Outer Hebrides; it also visits a couple of hidden sandy beaches. Currently owned by the National Trust for Scotland, Canna has an excellent café, campsite, guesthouse and honesty shop.

A Sanday puffin ▶

Canna

To Coroghan Castle

Distance 4.5km Time 1 hour 30
Terrain tracks and paths, rough at times
Map OS Explorer 397 Access Calmac ferry
from Mallaig

**This short introduction to Canna
explores the historic buildings and ruins
around the main settlement, A'Chill,
taking in views of Canna House and
Coroghan Castle.**

From the ferry jetty take the track
northwest, soon passing Rhu Church. Also
known as 'the Rocket Church' due to its
distinctive shape, it was based on an Irish
design and built in 1911 as a place of
worship for the Protestant Thom family
who owned the predominantly Catholic
Canna at that time; it saved them a 50km
trip by sea to the nearest alternative.
Although the church, dedicated to

St Columba, is still consecrated it is rarely
used today. Ignore a a track on the right to
carry straight on by the shore, passing the
island's café and then the tiny post office
crammed into a charming wooden shed.

Just beyond the Catholic chapel with a
white cross on the gable end, turn right
through a gate, following an orange
waymarker. Built after 1770 and also
dedicated to St Columba the chapel
served the Catholic population until
1897 when a large church on Sanday
replaced it. It spent some of the
intervening time serving as the island's
post office and shop before being brought
back into use for worship in 1965.

Keep to the grass track shadowing the
wall and then bending right before
entering a wood via an iron gate – you'll
find a mass of bluebells here in late

spring. Soon pass the grave of John Lorne Campbell, the Gaelic scholar who gifted Canna to the National Trust for Scotland.

Leave the wood by a gate into a field. Within a fenced enclosure are the remains of an early Christian cross dating from between the 7th and 9th centuries; it is missing its top and one arm, supposedly as a result of cannonball practice during the Napoleonic Wars. From here head to the prominent standing stone on top of a mound. The small indentation on its side was reputedly used to punish criminals – an offender's thumb would be jammed for a period of time befitting his (or her) crime. From the stone, head between a fence and a craggy mound, soon climbing a stile next to the old graveyard.

Keep left as you cross the field to go through a gate in the far corner and shortly rejoin the outward grassy track. Turn right and follow this back to the main island track by the farm. Turn left back along this and, after the phonebox, you come to the entrance to Canna House. Now owned by the National Trust for Scotland, the house is open on specific days but the gardens are always worth exploring.

Continue past the café and, immediately beyond the cottage, turn left through a gate to follow a path beside the walls of Canna House gardens and then through woodland. Follow the blue waymarkers as the path makes a twisting ascent through the trees before dropping to a gate. Go through this and cross the field diagonally to pass through a gate in the opposite corner, emerging near the island's telephone exchange. Another gate leads to a good viewpoint over Coroghan Castle set on its rocky crag. Used as a prison in the 17th century it is said that Marion Macleod was imprisoned here for being unfaithful to her husband. These days the structure is in a very dangerous condition so do not attempt to climb to it.

Go back through the gate and then left to enter another gate by a stone barn. From here you can detour down to the fine sandy beach, before following the track inland and turning left when it meets the main island track to return to the ferry pier.

The Souterrains

Distance 9.5km **Time** 3 hours 30
Terrain tracks, boggy, rough ground to
reach souterrains requiring map and
navigation skills **Map** OS Explorer 397
Access Calmac ferry from Mallaig

Canna is home to a collection of earth
houses, or souterrains, likely to have
been built in the Iron Age to store food
and possibly to serve as a place of refuge
during attack. This walk passes Canna
House before crossing moorland to
discover two of these fascinating
structures on the side of Beinn Tighe.

Starting from the pier follow the track
past the lovely Church of Scotland or
'Rocket Church' on the left before
eventually passing the island's café and
then Canna House. The gardens are worth
exploring and it is also possible to take a
tour of the house, home to the previous
owners of Canna, accomplished scholars
and folklorists, John Lorne Campbell and
Margaret Fay Shaw. Having spent much of
their lives collecting folklore and music
from the Highlands and developing
farming techniques on the island they
gifted the land to the National Trust for
Scotland in 1981.

The track serves as Canna's main
highway, although as it is a private road
local vehicles do not need an MOT or road
tax. Go past St Columba's Chapel and
some farm buildings where there is also a

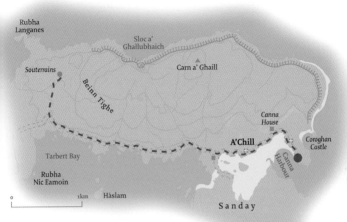

public toilet. Just before a cottage head right through a gate waymarked with a red arrow to follow the south coast of the island. The cliffs here are ideal for watching for golden and white-tailed eagles – the Small Isles have a healthy population of both. The track curves right and drops downhill with a sandy beach visible ahead. Where the track turns sharply to the left, leave it – a stone marker indicates a faint path aiming inland to the north here. The going can be boggy and it's best to keep an eye on the map for this section.

The ridged ground offers evidence of cultivation. These so-called lazy beds were anything but – crofters, usually women, would gather seaweed to carry in baskets on their backs in order to fertilise the wide strips of soil furrowed with drainage ditches. Steer west (left) of a small knoll

and continue on a vague track northwards. After crossing a wooden bridge keep left for a short time until the faint path splits; branch right, following tiny cairns as you climb the slope to the east. Carry on heading diagonally right and, after passing the remains of a drystane dyke, the entrances to the two souterrains can be found.

With care you can lower yourself into the stone-lined passage and feel the cool air – perfect for storing food, and the posh fridge of its day. Pieces of pottery have been found in the area and archaeologists believe other unexcavated souterrains or earth houses probably exist nearby. The way back is simply to return along the outward route to the ferry pier.

◀ Rum from Tarbert Bay

Sanday and the sea stacks

Distance 12.5km Time 4 hours
Terrain track, moorland, pathless and
boggy in places, dogs to be kept under
strict control Map OS Explorer 397
Access Calmac ferry from Mallaig

Neighbouring Sandy is joined to Canna by
a bridge; it is home to a thriving puffin
colony and some fine coastal cliffs, as well
as a small lighthouse and large church.

The puffins tend to arrive at their
breeding colonies on Sanday in April,
staying until mid August, helpfully
coinciding with the main tourist season
(such as it is on Canna!). Outwith these
months there is still much to see on this
route, with other seabirds and wildlife to
spot. Sanday is attached to Canna via a
bridge and it is first necessary to head
from the ferry pier through the settlement
of A'Chill and around the bay to get here.

Starting from the ferry pier, follow the
main track past the church with its rocket-
shaped tower and then the island café and
Canna House. Pass a farm and keep left at a
junction to stay next to the sea, eventually
reaching the bridge to Sanday – note the
small Catholic shrine as you arrive on the
island. Take the track to the left, ignoring
the new road heading inland which
replaced the tidal track in 2018. Pass some
houses and stay next to the sea at a fork to
continue on the track; it can be submerged
in places at high tide but it is usually
possible to get through with dry feet.

Beyond the primary school the track
skirts a small bay and heads inland after
the last house, passing through a gate – a
short detour here takes you to a headland
which is a good place to look for seals.
Soon you come to St Edward's Church.
This impressive building dates from 1890

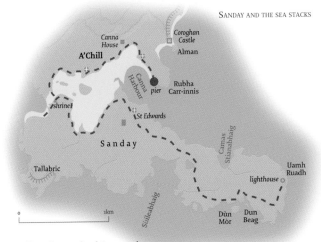

and was a gift to the people of Canna and Sanday from the 3rd Marchioness of Bute as a memorial to her father. The chapel in A'Chill was then converted to the post office and shop, and the Catholics on the island worshipped here until 1963. By then a sharply declining population and the effect of the harsh weather had taken its toll and the church was in such a state of disrepair that the Catholics re-opened the chapel on Canna and moved the post office to its current position. The church building is now listed and deconsecrated; it had a couple of further leases of life as a hostel and Gaelic Study Centre but today its vast space is empty.

Head through the gate in the drystane dyke ahead and, part way across the next field, turn left through a gateway in the wall, following a grassy track. Aim southeast over rough grazing ground – there is only a faint path – leading to a gate in the middle of a drystane dyke.

Now stay on the drier ground to the left of the bog, heading for the cliffs of the southern coast. Soon the impressive sea stacks of flat-topped Dun Mor and narrow Dun Beag come into view.

These are the breeding grounds for a sizeable puffin colony which themselves attract great skuas, the pirates of the skies, who will aggressively harass the puffins coming back to feed their hungry chicks into dropping their catch, which the skua will then polish off.

The route continues along the coast on a narrow path to reach the far end of Sanday and its small lighthouse – a fabulous viewpoint across to the Isle of Rum. Retrace your steps, but just before the bridge it is worth detouring a short distance on a grassy path along the coastline and through a gate to reach a small but beautiful sandy beach. Return to the ferry pier by your outward route.

◀ Dun Mor

Canna coastal compass

Distance 19.5km Time 9 hours
Terrain rough, pathless moor and grazing
land Map OS Explorer 397
Access Calmac ferry from Mallaig

**This is Canna's wildest and most
challenging walk – a circumnavigation on
foot. It takes in wild clifftops, fertile
farmland and rugged moorland with sea
and mountain views at every turn.**

From the ferry take the track towards
the main village, soon passing the
distinctive rocket-shaped tower of
St Columba's Church. Take the next right
onto a walled track and, immediately
before a farm building, go through a gate
on the left. Aim right through the field to
another gate in front of the telephone
exchange building. You can detour

through the gate for a good view of
Coroghan Castle atop its high crag, but
you would need to return back through
the gate and follow the fence uphill.
At the top go through another gate and
bear right, still climbing uphill.

You can either pass to the left of the
craggy escarpment of Compass Hill or
detour to the right to climb to the top.
The hill is so named as its magnetic rock
is said to be strong enough to affect the
compasses of ships out at sea. To bypass
the hill, continue northwards across a
grassy hollow to meet the fence along the
northern cliffs. Here, on a clear day, the
views of the Cuillin mountains on Skye
are exceptional.

Follow the fence to the left. The rough
terrain is rewarded by spectacular cliff

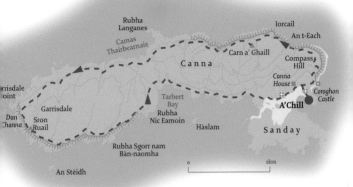

Iorcail
An t-Each
Rubha
Langanes
Camas
Thairbearnais
Carn a' Ghaill
Canna
Compass
Hill
Canna
House
Rubha
Nic Eamoin
Tarbert
Bay
Coroghon
Castle
A'CHILL
Garrisdale
isdale
oint
Dun
Channa
Sron
Ruail
Hàslam
Sanday
Rubha Sgorr nam
Bàn-naomha
An Stèidh

0   2km

views. While there is no formal path, faint
sheep trods ease the going in places – just
ensure you stay well back from the cliffs.
It is necessary to detour inland around a
couple of fenced inlets – after the second
of these head directly across the
moorland to detour to the highest point
on Canna, Carn a'Ghaill. Topped by a trig
point and standing at 211m above the sea,
its commanding views sweep over the
neighbouring islands. From here aim
northwest to rejoin the clifftop and follow
a fence over Beinn Tighe. The route
descends steeply in a couple of places
as it continues over Buidhe Sgorr.

A third steep descent leads to the
low-lying narrow neck at the centre of
Canna. Keep following the fence to reach
a stile and then head down to a gate in
a drystane dyke. Rejoin the coastline,
soon carefully crossing over a stone wall
where it abuts a fence by the sea.
Immediately after this, bear left steeply

up grass to begin the clifftop walk around
Canna's western half.

The terrain is largely grassy but it is wet
in places. An inlet forces you inland to a
stile and a dip; a sandy beach can be
viewed from the cliff before you reach the
western end of the island. From here the
going becomes easier, keeping high above
the shoreline fort of Dun Channa to reach
the dramatically-situated trig point on
Sron Ruail. The cliffs now turn eastwards
with a number of steep descents and
climbs to tackle.

When you come to grazing land the
route goes through a gate in a drystane
dyke, then aims for another gate just to
the right of the farm buildings at Tarbert.
Cross a field to reach a track, then take this
to pass around Tarbert Bay before heading
uphill, later descending near the grassy
shore. A gate by a cottage gives access to
the main A'Chill track which takes you
past the island's farm, post office and café
on the way back to the start.

◀ Looking over Sanday from the cliffs

Low-lying and hidden from the mainland, Coll is surprisingly rugged and rocky, and ringed by some of the most beautiful secluded sandy beaches in all the Hebrides. The island was used as the inspiration for the Katie Morag books by Mairi Hedderwick which, although penned more than 25 years ago, still enthral youngsters with their tales of young Katie's visits to her grandmother's island home. Coll is now served by a roll-on roll-off car ferry, but if you want to recreate the pre-car feel of Katie Morag's era, bikes are available for hire from the post office in Arinagour – the island can fairly easily be explored with a combination of two wheels and on foot.

Knobbly Coll offers a more diverse landscape than its flatter more fertile neighbour Tiree. A number of short walks give access to small beaches, rocky coves and dune landscapes offering good places to picnic, swim or wildlife watch. The RSPB reserve at Totronald is the place to go to try and spot the elusive corncrake, though you're more likely to hear its rasping call than catch a sighting. Two impressive castles from different eras can be seen on the walk at Breachacha, whilst older forts and Iron Age remains are visible on a number of routes. The highest summit, Ben Hogh, seems a lot tougher than its diminutive 106m height suggests, but it is the place to go for 360-degree views across the island.

Cliad Bay ▶

Coll

Beaches of the far west

Distance 12.75km **Time** 3 hours 30
Terrain grassy machair, beaches, some
pathless and boggy stretches. Grazing
livestock and nesting terns, so keep dogs
on tight leads **Map** OS Explorer 372
Access Calmac ferry from Oban and Tiree
docks 1km south of Arinagour

**Explore the westernmost tip of Coll
taking in the stunning Feall and
Crossapol Beaches and part of the RSPB's
Coll nature reserve.**

Begin from the parking area on the
machair at the far end of the public road
in the southwest of the island, keeping
left on the B8070 after Uig. If walking from
Arinagour on the link loop, the route can
be joined at Arileod. Start by taking the
grassy track signed for Feall Bay and head
north, keeping to the left of a fence. This
is part of the RSPB nature reserve which
provides a unique habitat for barnacle and
white-fronted geese in the winter,
lapwing, redshank and snipe in spring
and the rare corncrake in the summer.
There are also breeding terns nearer
Calgary Point, so please ensure you do
not disturb any nesting sites, detour away
from the birds if they start alarm calling,
and either avoid bringing dogs during the
breeding season (April to August) or keep
them on a short lead.

At a fork in the track you can make a
short detour to the top of Ben Feall for
fantastic views by carrying straight on,
then return to this spot; otherwise take
the left fork. The route soon crosses the
1km stretch of fine sand that is Traigh
Feall. From the far end, head up to a fence,
turning right along it for a short while
before going through a walkers' gate.

A grassy track now aims westwards to
reach a footpath marker post after some
time. As the coastline curves to the left

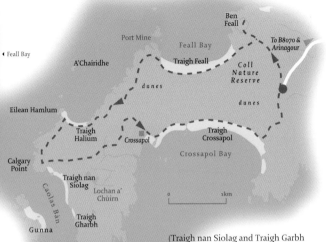

◀ Feall Bay

stay on a vague path a little way back from the sea, eventually reaching a footpath junction sign. Turn right, signposted for Calgary Point, go through a gate in a fence and cross rougher, wetter ground. Carry on in the same direction beyond another marker post and climb a stile over a fence to soon emerge on a second beach – Traigh Halium.

Once across this, take a grassy track west to a gate and continue round the coastline towards Calgary Point. A trig point provides an excellent viewpoint overlooking the Isle of Gunna in the sound between Coll and Tiree. To the south are yet more magnificent beaches

(Traigh nan Siolag and Traigh Garbh which can be visited on a long detour), but this route makes a more direct return, bearing due east from the trig, at first aiming for a wind turbine. After a gate in a fence, continue in the same direction to reach another gate at a corner. Go through this and follow the fence on the left to avoid the worst of the boggy ground, still heading east before bearing north to join a clear stony track. After passing through a gate, the track eventually bends right and goes past some agricultural sheds before reaching the farmhouse at Crossapol. From here it leads down to a cemetery and then onto the sands at the west end of Traigh Crossapol, arguably the finest of the many beaches on Coll. Bear left to cross the sands, backed by high dunes for almost the entire 2km. Here a sandy track heads inland; take this to return to the parking area at the start.

Breachacha Castles and Ben Feall

Distance **6km** Time **1 hour 30**
Terrain **grassy tracks, short climb, small
boggy section** Map **OS Explorer 372**
Access **Calmac ferry from Oban and Tiree
docks 1km south of Arinagour**

**A small hilltop on western Coll offers
some truly stunning vistas; from it the
walk passes the two contrasting castles
at Breachacha, once home to the
Macleans of Coll.**

Take the B8070 to Arileod, turning left at
the T-junction here and continuing to the
end of the road. There is a small parking
area on the machair here. Start by
following a grassy track, signed for Feall
Bay, northwards, keeping left of a fence.

Much of this land is owned and
managed by the RSPB. It provides a winter
home to barnacle and white-fronted
geese, with lapwing, redshank and snipe
in the spring as well. You might also hear
the elusive corncrake in the summer
months; listen for it around the nettles
and yellow flag iris in the wetter areas
– it has a loud rasping call but is difficult
to spot. Climb the slope of Ben Feall,
ignoring tracks in other directions. As the
ground rises the views begin to open out
across the bay.

Once you gain the diminutive summit,
the full extent of this fantastic viewpoint is
laid out before you. Whilst only 66m above
the sea, it looks out across Feall Bay and
the rocky coastline further east, together
with both of the castles at Breachacha. The
eastern slope of this hill is too rocky to
make a pleasant descent, so instead start

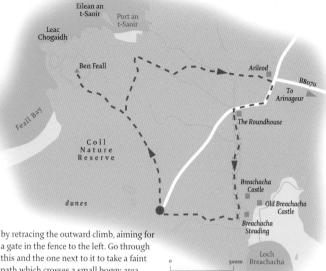

Eilean an t-Saoir
Port an t-Saoir
Leac Chogaidh
Ben Feall
Arileod
B8070
To Arinagour
The Roundhouse
Feall Bay
Coll Nature Reserve
Breachacha Castle
Old Breachacha Castle
dunes
Breachacha Steading
Loch Breachacha
0   500m

by retracing the outward climb, aiming for a gate in the fence to the left. Go through this and the one next to it to take a faint path which crosses a small boggy area, aiming for the tiny bay of Port an t-Saoir.

The route now heads east, shortly joining a track which leads through a gate to finally meet the road at Arileod. Turn right along this as it heads southwards and then bends right. After the Roundhouse, turn left onto a track, following a line of telegraph poles southwards. To the left is the 'New' Breachacha Castle, dating from the 1750s. Once home to the Macleans of Coll, it was built to replace the older 15th-century towerhouse known as the 'Old' Castle and has an impressive Georgian exterior. However, this wasn't enough to impress Samuel Johnson on his grand tour of the Hebrides in 1773 – driven from Coll by wild weather, he dismissed the house as a

'tradesman's box'. Both are private residences, the Old Castle now spectacularly restored, so please respect the privacy of the residents.

To best view the Old Castle, detour left from the track just before the old stable buildings. Cross some boggy ground and go through a gate to emerge on the open grassy ground leading down to the castle and the beach, but do not approach the private grounds of the castle itself. Afterwards return to the track and continue for a very short way to a gate giving access to the private yards of the old stable cottages. Turn right here, going through a gate to follow a rough track back to the parking area at the start.

◀ Mull's Ben More over the Breachacha Castles

Hogh Bay from Totronald

Distance 4km Time 1 hour
Terrain easy sandy tracks and beaches
Map OS Explorer 372
Access Calmac ferry from Oban and Tiree
docks 1km south of Arinagour

The chance of an encounter with the elusive corncrake may be the temptation for some, but the stunning sandy beach makes this walk worthwhile in any season.

The route starts from the parking area at the road end at Totronald, just beyond the RSPB information centre. It is worth visiting the information centre on the reserve to check up on recent sightings and head onto the viewing platform from where you might – just might – spot a corncrake. The corncrake begins to arrive from overwintering in Africa in mid-April

and will usually stay until late August or early September. It is much easier to hear its rasping 'krek krek' call, which is where its name comes from, than to catch sight of the small brown moorhen-like bird, which tend to hide in patches of nettles, flag iris or other undergrowth. Once numerous all over Britain, they tend to nest in arable crop fields so went into dramatic decline with the introduction of mechanised farming and crops which are cut at times when the birds have traditionally nested. Conservation schemes have introduced measures to ensure crofting practices provide a habitat for corncrakes; the population on Coll is slowly increasing.

From the car park begin the walk proper by heading through the gate and out along the grassy track onto the machair.

◂ Sands of Hogh Bay

In winter this area is home to a large number of barnacle and white-fronted geese who come here having spent the spring and summer in breeding grounds in Greenland and other northern climes. Keep left at a fork and then left again, passing between two small boulders. Soon the fine sand of Traigh Hogh comes into view, a beach which never fails to look spectacular whatever the weather or season. Aim for the far end of the bay, exploring the sands as you go.

Here, just before the rocky headland, there is a small burn. Cross this and

follow a faint path alongside it, heading inland. This soon reaches a grassy track beneath a row of telegraph poles. Turn right onto this and follow it back to the start. On this section in the spring and summer you may well see groundnesting lapwing and also redshank, so-named for their vivid red legs.

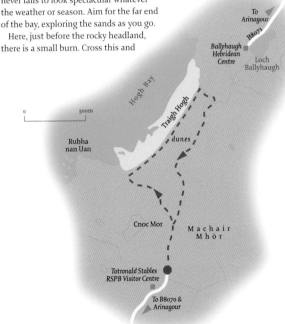

Ben Hogh and the Queen's Stone

Distance 1.5km **Time** 1 hour
Terrain indistinct paths, rough and
boggy in places **Map** OS Explorer 372
Access Calmac ferry from Oban and
Tiree docks 1km south of Arinagour

**Although only 106m high, Ben Hogh
is the highest summit on Coll and
an excellent vantage point. The climb
also visits the Clach na Ban-righ, a
massive boulder perched atop three
tiny stones.**

Start from the small group of cottages
at Clabhach where there is a sharp bend
in the road. If parking nearby, take great
care not to block entrances or passing
places – you can arrive on foot by way of

the central link loop from Arinagour.

Begin through the gate at the corner of
the road and follow the grassy track which
climbs southwards towards Ben Hogh.

The track soon narrows to a small
grassy path, aiming slightly right before
heading for the foot of the hill where a
wooden stile leads over a drystane dyke.
Now the path climbs steeply up the
heathery slopes but fades out as the
gradient eases.

You can't really miss the massive
boulder of the Clach na Ban-righ, or
Queen's Stone. A glacial erratic, this rock
was dragged and deposited here by a
slowly retreating glacier at the end of the
last ice age. The way it teeters on three
much smaller stones is at first
disconcerting, but it has been this way for
many thousands of years so it is unlikely
to become dislodged anytime soon.

James Boswell and Samuel Johnson came here in October 1773 as part of their tour of the Hebrides. Boswell wrote of it in *A Journal of A Tour to the Hebrides with Samuel Johnson*, noting, '*We passed by a place where there is a very large stone, I may call it a rock; – a vast weight for Ajax. The tradition is that a giant threw such another stone at his mistress, up to the top of a hill, at a small distance; and that she in return, threw this mass down to him. It was all in sport.*

As we advanced, we came to a large extent of plain ground. I had not seen such a place for a long time. Col [the Laird] and I took a gallop upon it by way of race. It was very refreshing to me, after having been so long taking short steps in hilly countries'.

From this point the summit trig point is indeed a short gallop away. Views extend in all directions, including many peaks on the Outer Hebrides on a clear day. The true summit is actually just to the southeast but this fact is unlikely to trouble anyone but the most ardent hillbagger. In case you are interested, Ben Hogh is designated as a 'hump' (hills of any height with a drop of 100m or more on all sides) and also as a 'tump' which must have a height difference of at least 30m on all sides.

Return by the same outward route to the cottages at Clabhach.

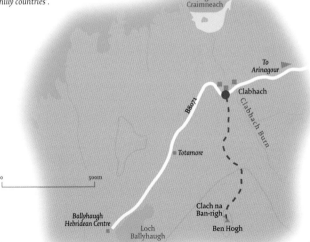

Heart of Coll link loop

Distance 20km **Time** 5 hours 30
Terrain mainly quiet minor roads, section
of sandy track **Map** OS Explorer 372
Access Calmac ferry from Oban and Tiree
docks 1km south of Arinagour

Coll is a great island to visit without a car
and this walk links together the start
points for some of the other shorter
walks on the island, making it possible
to spend a fuller day exploring. Although
the route is mainly on minor roads
these are very quiet and the landscape
is always attractive.

Start from Arinagour with its
whitewashed terraced houses. This is the
main settlement on Coll and is home to
most of the 200 islanders. Aim north
along the street, passing the café, two
shops and the signs for the island's hotel
to the right and community centre and
bunkhouse to the left. At a fork in the

road branch left, signed for the airport.
The quiet road now crosses open
moorland sprinkled with freshwater lochs
and lochans, passing the tiny airstrip after
about 7km – from here there are regular
flights to Oban and Tiree. At the road
junction at Arileod it is possible to join
the Breachacha Castles or the Calgary
Point routes by turning left. If continuing
on the central link loop, turn right here.

The next port of call is the RSPB
Totronald Visitor Centre, well worth a
visit to learn about this important wildlife
habitat that provides a summer home to
corncrakes, as well as a wealth of plants,
overwintering geese and groundnesting
birds. Just a little further along the road a
raised platform offers visitors the chance
to spot, or more likely hear, corncrakes
between April and late August.

From the car park go through a gate
onto a sandy track. Where the track forks,

◄ Arinagour

you can detour to the stunning beach at Hogh Bay by branching left on a grassy track; otherwise continue ahead on the main track. Soon this emerges at the Hebridean Centre at Ballyhaugh, home to a charity organising gap years overseas for young volunteers. Keep to the right of the buildings, going through two gates to reach the surfaced road.

From here, you'll see Coll's highest hill, Ben Hogh, on the far side of a lochan. To detour up to this fantastic little viewpoint, continue for 1km until

the road arrives at Clabhach where the ascent route is picked up. Otherwise carry on along the road to pass the signed track for Cliad Bay (also worth a detour) until you reach the road junction at Arnabost.

Bear right here for the final 3.5km stretch of road. There are lovely views over the long inlet of Loch Eatharna as you approach Arinagour to complete your island circuit.

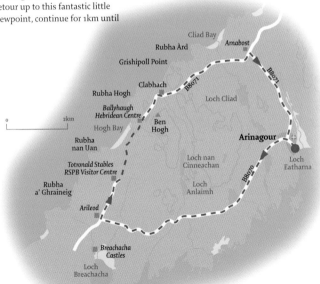

Cliad Bay and the northwest

**Distance 9.25km Time 3 hours 30
Terrain beaches, grassy paths, minor
road, pathless hill Map OS Explorer 372
Access Calmac ferry from Oban and Tiree
docks 1km south of Arinagour**

**Discover perfect sandy beaches, look
out for seals and climb a tiny rock peak
on this exploration of Coll's wild
western coast.**

The walk starts near Cliad, soon after
the B8071 from Arinagour turns left at a
T-junction at Arnabost on the north side
of the island. There is limited parking
where a track signed for Cliad Bay leaves
to the north of the road. Begin by going
through a gate and over grazing land to
pass the island's recycling centre.

Continue on what is now a grassy track
leading through the dunes and down
onto Cliad Bay's sandy beach.

It is unusual for there to be another
person on this fine beach, although hardy
surfers seek it out when the conditions
are right. Its tranquillity is one of the
reasons seals choose these rocks to haul
out at low tide; dolphins have also been
spotted playing in the waters here. There
are great views over to the Outer Hebrides
on a clear day.

Aim to the right across the sands,
crossing a small burn. At the far end of
the beach head up the grass, crossing a
stile over a fence. Beyond, the springy
machair comes alive with flowers, insects
and birds in the summer months; cross

this and pass a much smaller beach with its own tidal islet offshore. The route bears east now on a vague path before eventually a grassy track leads to a gate in a fence. Once through this, head towards the sand of Bagh an Trailleich. A gate gives access down to another stretch of pristine sand. Keep heading in the same direction to cross the bay; a short rocky scramble at the far side leads back up onto the machair. Here, a faint grassy track follows the coastline, leading through another gate at one point.

In a while yet another stunning sweep of sand comes into view – Traigh Gharbh. Carry straight on to cross a grassy area and reach a deeper sandy inlet. From here you can see the next objective, the small rock peak further along the coast.

After crossing the sands of the inlet, aim northeast across rougher grassland to reach the foot of this miniature peak, A' Chroic, standing at 40m high. The climb to the summit is a short rocky scramble but is worth the effort for the fabulous views along this rugged Coll coastline.

After soaking up the view, retrace your steps down from A' Chroic before bearing south to join the road. Turn right and follow this very quiet road for around 4km to the start, keeping straight on at the Arnabost junction.

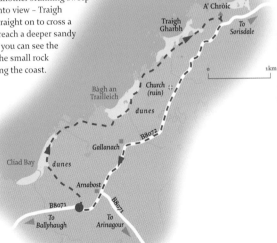

Dun Morbhaidh and the machair

Distance 1km **Time** 1 hour
Terrain pathless, grassy, short climb
to fort **Map** OS Explorer 372
Access Calmac ferry from Oban and Tiree
docks 1km south of Arinagour

Head across the richly diverse machair
grassland to reach the site of an old Iron
Age fort above a beautiful stretch of
coastline. This short walk then continues
by exploring the sandy beach.

Finding the start of this walk is likely to
be your biggest challenge. Head towards
the northern end of the island and, before
you get as far as Bousd, look out for a
wooden post beside the B8072 at the
point where the rough ground on the
north side of the road changes to smooth
grass (GR NM236629). From here, an

indistinct grassy track leads across the
turf with a fence to its left. Stick with the
fence when it runs to the left, keeping
between the fence and a rocky outcrop as
you head towards the sea.

Soon the rocky hillock of Dun
Morbhaidh comes into view ahead. Climb
the rough steep ground for views along
the intricate Coll coastline. Only a few
traces of the walls of the fort remain on
the west side. The fort was partially
excavated in 1903 by linen manufacturer,
antiquarian and archaeologist Erskine
Beveridge, who found a number of
hammerstones and some pottery
fragments inscribed with images of deer;
these are currently displayed at the
National Museum of Scotland in
Edinburgh. Similar pieces have been

◄ View from Dun Morbhaidh

found at other sites around both the Inner and Outer Hebrides.

The coastline is worth exploring in either direction here; this route heads to the small sandy beach just to the east of the Dun from which it is a straightforward walk back across the machair to the start point. 'Machair' is the Gaelic name given to these low-lying fertile plains. The term is used to describe coastal dunes that have been cultivated and other land lying between the sandy coast and the peat which lies further inland. Traditionally this fairly narrow crofting strip was fertilised by annual applications of seaweed and traditionally used to raise barley, oats, rye and potatoes. Due to the high shell content of the thin soil, the machair has developed into a unique and diverse habitat, supporting a wide range of wildflowers, insects and birdlife. In Coll small damp patches of machair are home to Europe's rarest orchid, the cream-coloured Irish Lady's Tresses.

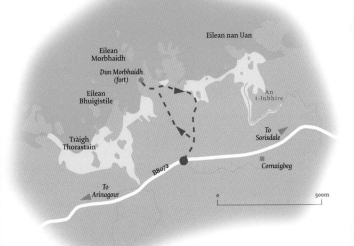

Sorisdale to Traigh Tuath

Distance 2.75km **Time** 1 hour
Terrain grass path, sandy beach, pathless
dunes **Map** OS Explorer 372
Access Calmac ferry from Oban and Tiree
docks 1km south of Arinagour

**Explore the magical northernmost part
of Coll, wandering through near-deserted
croft settlements before reaching some
glorious sandy beaches.**

At the far end of the public road (B8072)
at the north end of the island there is a
turning area; it is usually possible to find
somewhere to park carefully without
obstructing this or blocking access.
Continue on foot down the track that
takes over where the road ends. Go
through a gate, passing a sign for the bay
and north shore. Carry on along the track,
branching right at a fork to pass through
the remains of the crofting and fishing
village. A mixture of ruined old thatched

houses stands amidst more modern
properties with only a handful of mainly
part-time residents.

Pass the gable-end of the last house and
head down onto the beautiful sandy
beach, bearing left across it to soon reach
the grassy ground at the back of the bay.
After passing through a gate, you can
detour to the headland by turning right,
going through a gap in a ruined wall and
following the path out to the point with
views across the sea to Mull's highest
mountain, Ben More.

Return almost as far as the gate, but
turn right before you reach it to follow
the fenceline. When the track bends right
towards a private house, keep straight on
by the fence, soon crossing rougher
ground. Nearing the sea, cross a wooden
boardwalk and go through a gate to enter
an area of dunes. An ancient burial site
was excavated in the dunes in the 1970s

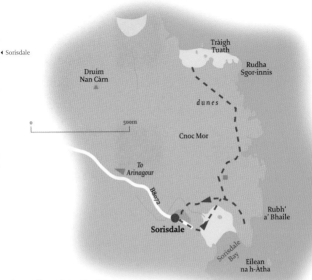

◀ Sorisdale

Tràigh
Tuath

Rudha
Sgor-innis

Druim
Nan Càrn

dunes

Cnoc Mor

0   500m

To
Arinagour

B8072

Sorisdale

Rubh'
a' Bhaile

*Sorisdale
Bay*

Eilean
na h-Àtha

and a number of shards of Beaker pottery were found, as well as a body which was dated to around 1930BC; it is thought there may have been a dwelling dating from that period in this area as well. A number of faint paths run through the dunes to reach the stunning sands of the very secluded Traigh Tuath. This is a perfect summer picnic spot and pretty special in most weather.

Just a little way east along the coast, at the headland of Rubha Mor, was the site of Coll's very own *Whisky Galore*. Here, in poor weather in July 1942, the *Nevada* ran aground whilst sailing in a convoy of six World War II vessels bound for West Africa. It is said that locals made the most of the illicit bounty, which included cigarettes, alcohol, hair oil and other goods, evading the official salvagers and supposedly hiding the odd whisky bottle in nearby rabbit holes. The whereabouts of some of the 10 cases of West African banknotes remains a mystery to this day, although there were reports of banknotes being found among the dunes and of a local crofter drying wads of them alongside his crops until he found they had no value and turned them in. The wreck is still visited by divers, but marine life rather than hidden treasure is the attraction these days. The best return route is to retrace your steps to Sorisdale and the start.

Tiree often claims to have record sunshine levels – and it is certainly true that this low-lying, most westerly of Inner Hebridean isles often avoids the clouds that can envelop the mountains of nearby Skye and Mull. You're quite likely to leave with a tan, at least from the neck up, as the island is reliably windy, resulting in stunning sandy beaches that provide the perfect backdrop for wind- and wave-surfers alike. The laid-back surfer vibe lends itself to relaxed holidays enjoying the scenery and wildlife with the annual music festival now a big draw. It is also gaining a reputation as an active destination, with its numerous walks joined by cycling, watersports and running, including an annual ultramarathon, much of which is over sand (quite an achievement on an island that's only 17km long by 10km wide).

Tiree traditionally made its living from crofting, but tourism is now a substantial earner. During the Second World War a large number of RAF servicemen were stationed on the island and the radar station on Beinn Hough still operates, although these days the stunning view from the top is the main attraction. An earlier form of communication can be explored on the Hynish walk, which starts from the beautiful harbour and lighthouse keepers' cottages to visit the relay station built for the massive Skerryvore Lighthouse which stands 19km out to sea. Other walks skim the beautiful coastline with its impressive beaches, craggy cliffs and dunes, as well as the traditional architecture unique to Tiree.

On the road by Traigh Mhor ▶

Tiree

Dun Mor Broch and the Ringing Stone

Distance 9.75km Time 3 hours 30
Terrain minor road, pathless coast
walking, sandy beach Map OS Explorer
372 Access Calmac ferry from Oban, Ring-
n-Ride request bus on Tiree

**This superb circuit takes in Tiree's most
interesting archaeological features,
including a well-preserved fortified broch
and the Ringing Stone which was marked
with carvings over 4500 years ago.**

There is limited parking on the verge of
the B8069 at the west end of Traigh Mhor
bay, keeping east of the cattle grid. Start
by walking west along the road and right
at the junction, signposted for Gott.
Continue to the end of the surfaced road,
aiming diagonally across the trackless
grass and keeping to the left of the last
white cottage. Soon the route joins a
rough track which leads along the
southwest shore of Loch Riaghain. After
two gates the track passes between a pair
of lochans and then meets a fence. Leave
the track here and turn right to follow the
fence to the coast. From this point the
route is pathless but continues in the
same direction to cross the grassy machair
with the sea on your left.

Very soon the Ringing Stone comes into
view near the shoreline. This massive
boulder has cup-marked carvings thought
to have been made by the Beaker people
4500 years ago. When lightly struck with a
small stone the boulder is said to make a
metallic ringing sound – hence the name.
Obviously this has been a very special
stone to people for thousands of years, so
help preserve it by treating it very gently.

From the stone carry on along the grass
backing the rocky shore to reach a sandy
beach after 1km. Look out for concrete
steps set into the drystane dyke and cross
here before bearing northeast up grassy
and often boggy ground, aiming between
two rocky outcrops.

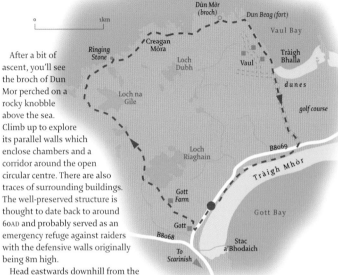

After a bit of ascent, you'll see the broch of Dun Mor perched on a rocky knobble above the sea. Climb up to explore its parallel walls which enclose chambers and a corridor around the open circular centre. There are also traces of surrounding buildings. The well-preserved structure is thought to date back to around 60AD and probably served as an emergency refuge against raiders with the defensive walls originally being 8m high.

Head eastwards downhill from the broch, crossing the back of the next inlet and aiming for a gate. Go through this into a grassy field with a tiny cottage and climb the obvious flat-topped mound of Dun Beag. The remains of this fort are probably older than the broch; little remains visible on the ground, although the great location can be appreciated with views in many directions. Clamber down from Dun Beag and aim southeast along the coastline of Vaul Bay.

After a rockier section the route runs along a grassy path that leads to the shore. Head between two stone gateposts before emerging at the west end of beautiful Traigh Bhalla, where a track and then a minor road are reached by some restored Tiree-style houses. The traditional style had a high boat-like roof draining into a sand-filled gap between the two stone walls. At the road bear south back across the island with Vaul Golf Course on your left – here the sheep keep all but the greens in order with their grazing.

On reaching the T-junction with the B8069, you can turn right to walk back to the start or cross to the beautiful sands of Traigh Mhor and bear right for a barefoot beach. Traigh Mhor is home to the Tiree Wave Classic, a prestigious windsurfing contest held every October.

Caolas explorer

Distance 8.25km Time 3 hours
Terrain sometimes muddy tracks, minor
road, path to beach Map OS Explorer 372
Access Calmac ferry from Oban, Ring-n-
Ride request bus on Tiree

A lovely circuit explores the
eastern part of the island, taking in
the obligatory stunning sandy beach,
this one with grandstand views over
Gunna Sound.

Start from Salum, where there is limited
parking on the verge before the road end.
Head north to the end of the road and
continue along the track, keeping to the
left of a white farmhouse. After a gateway,
continue along the grassy track which
soon approaches the shore and a view to
the tidal islet of Fadamull.

Stay on the clear track, passing through
a gate and then following a grassy ridge.

After running alongside a fence, it then
swings left in an area of open ground.
Beyond another gate you reach the
farmhouse at Miodar. Pass round this to
the right (or alternatively left through a
gate) to reach the access track for the
house and follow this as it bears east.

A T-junction gives you the opportunity
to detour to the beach. If it's very high
tide or you don't want to visit the beach
turn right to stay on the track, otherwise
carry straight on over the open ground,
keeping left of a house, to reach a gate
giving access to the shore. Beyond this,
turn right along the shore.

Cross the beach until your way is
blocked by a headland topped by a fence.
Dive inland here to cross the machair by
the fence and rejoin the road. Turn left
and at the next T-junction turn right and
then left, signposted for Milton. Follow

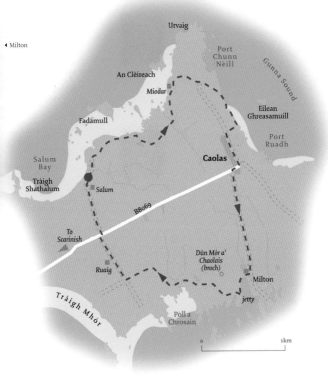

this back road for a little over 1km until you reach a white house on the right, overlooking the sea. Turn right to pass the front of the house and follow the track to the Milton jetty.

After passing through the gate just beyond the jetty, leave the main track by bearing sharp right to follow an indistinct track which can be very muddy at first. This soon doubles back and then mirrors

the coast behind the next inlet as the terrain improves underfoot. Raised on an embankment, the track passes a lochan before meandering across the rugged ground. Eventually it goes through a gate in a drystane dyke and continues as a walled lane. Stay on this to reach a road and turn right to pass through Ruaig. At a staggered junction turn right and then left onto the Salum road to return to the start.

Loch Bhasapoll to Traigh Chornaig

Distance 3.25km **Time** 1 hour
Terrain minor roads, sandy beach,
pathless machair **Map** OS Explorer 372
Access Calmac ferry from Oban, Ring-n-
Ride request bus on Tiree

**Watch the windsurfers on Loch Bhasapoll
before setting off on a bracing walk to
the spectacular beach of Traigh Chornaig
on Tiree's north coast.**

Begin from the car park on the north
side of Loch Bhasapoll. Being windy and
sunny Tiree is a popular destination for
watersports such as windsurfing and
kitesurfing and the loch is often busy
with groups and individuals practising
their skills.

From the loch, start by walking west
along the minor road and then branching
right along a well-made track. Cross a
cattle grid and aim for a white cottage
overlooking the bay. Here the fence on the
right ends, allowing access down over the
dunes to the right to reach the far end of
the sands of Traigh Chornaig.

This is a truly magnificent beach. Cross

the shell sand until you reach the first of several broken lines of rock extending seaward (around three-quarters of the way along the beach). Now walk up the dunes to reach a stile in the fence.

Beyond the stile, the route heads inland across the machair and grazing land, aiming for the red phonebox in the distance. As you near this, pass in front of a white house, keeping it on your right, and join a track. This leads to a gate giving access to the road. Turn right to follow the road past the school, turning right again at a T-junction to return to the start.

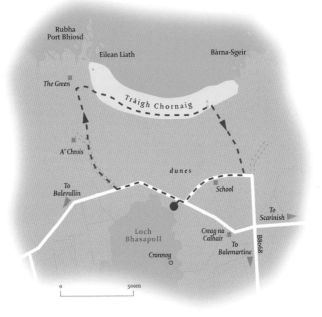

Heanish horseshoe

Distance 2km **Time** 1 hour **Terrain** grassy paths, sandy beach **Map** OS Explorer 372 **Access** Calmac ferry from Oban, Ring-n-Ride request bus on Tiree

This short walk crosses the machair to visit the site of an Iron Age fort and the beautiful sandy bay of Traigh an Duin.

Start from Heanish, a small group of houses approximately 1km to the west of Scarinish. There is only very limited parking nearby, so make sure you don't block any entrances or passing places – alternatively you could walk to the start along the road from Scarinish.

From the middle of the small group of houses making up Heanish, walk west along the road and turn left through a gate into a grassy field with a white bungalow and telegraph pole in it.

There are still a few traditional houses built in the vernacular style unique to Tiree dotted across the island. These crofters' houses were built using a double wall of stone laid without any mortar and with a gap between the two walls which

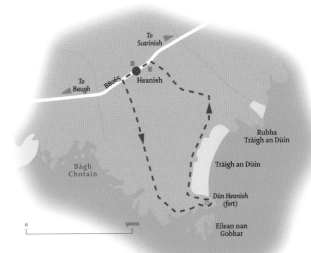

was filled with sand. The roof beams are supported by the inner wall so that rainwater runs down the marram grass thatch and into the layer of sand. The thatch was usually held down by weighted stones and would be replaced every couple of years. The double wall and thatch forms the distinctive shape of the Tiree houses.

Cross the field, passing in front of the bungalow and keeping to the right of another old house. Stay to the left of a fence to soon emerge on the rocky coastline, bearing left towards the low mound of Dun Heanish. The remains of the circular stone walls of the fort are now just grassy mounds but the strategic

value of the site remains apparent, with excellent views. An ancient midden, or rubbish dump, was exposed here by coastal erosion and found to contain pottery, hammerstones, pot boilers, shells and bones. A large bowl hollowed from a rock was also found locally and thought to date back to the period of the fort.

From the Dun, dip down onto the pristine sand of Traigh an Duin, the Beach of the Fort, and cross as far as the wood-panelled house near the far end. Skirt around the far side of the house to join its access track and follow this back to a gate and the road in Heanish.

Hough Bay and Beinn

**Distance 5.5km Time 2 hours 30
Terrain grassy track, sandy beach, rough,
boggy moorland Map OS Explorer 372
Access Calmac ferry from Oban, Ring-n-
Ride request bus on Tiree**

**Cross the machair towards the sublime
beaches that fringe Tiree's most westerly
point, before tackling the rough climb to
the southern summit of Beinn Hough.**

The walk starts from the minor
road south of Beinn Hough where there
are a couple of houses and some limited
verge parking. Set out along the
signposted footpath for the shore from
here. At a fork in front of a bungalow take
the middle of three tracks. This grassy
track leads over the machair to a gate in a
fence. Follow the fence to the left to reach
a footpath sign and walkers' gate; go
through this and continue with the fence
on your left.

When you meet another grassy track,
turn right onto it aiming for the headland
of Rubha Hanais. Work your way around
the corner of a fence and across the grass
towards a low mound – Dun Hanais – the
site of an ancient fort. Little remains of
the stonework but the mound provides
the perfect viewpoint for the stunning
sweep of Traigh Thodhrasdail to the
south. It is possible to detour to the sands
through a nearby gate.

Otherwise continue along the grassy
coastline to the north, skirting around the
back of the small bay of Port Hanais,
passing through a gate and then
continuing on a grassy track leading out
onto Rubha Chraiginis. This is the most
westerly point on Tiree. From here aim
down to the next beach, Traigh Hough.
Cross the sand to reach more rocky and
pebbly ground. At this point, divert inland
to join a good track which meanders

◄ Traigh Thodhrasdail

eastwards through the dunes. When you emerge onto an area of flat machair, bear southeast across the grassy ground, keeping to the right of the concrete building and aiming for the dip at the centre of Beinn Hough ahead.

The ascent of Beinn Hough is rough, steep and boggy and can be omitted by contouring around its base to the right. To climb to the top, cross the boggy ground to the Bealach na Beinne, the dip between the hill's northern and southern peaks. If you want to climb to the

northern summit – the second highest point on Tiree – detour northeast from here. This route climbs the lower southern summit because it's such a splendid viewpoint. From the bealach keep bearing south over rough and, at first, very steep ground to reach the mast. Here the whole of Tiree is spread out beneath you, almost flat apart from its three hills.

To descend, follow the road down from the larger mast. This soon leads back to the road at the start of the walk.

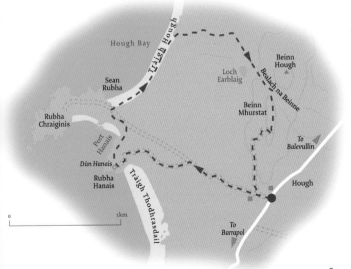

Coast of Ceann a'Mhara

Distance 5.5km **Time** 2 hours 30
Terrain beach, rocky, pathless coast and
grassy machair **Map** OS Explorer 372
Access Calmac ferry from Oban, Ring-n-
Ride request bus on Tiree

**Escape the flat lands of Tiree with
this exploration of the wild and rugged
Ceann a'Mhara headland. Fantastic
coastal scenery and an approach across
a wonderful beach make this walk
a Tiree classic.**

Begin from the parking area just south
of Loch a'Phuill which is reached via a
track from Meningie – stop at the first
fenced parking area rather than driving
over the machair. From here the bird
hides on the opposite side of the track
can be visited – great for watching overwintering geese on the loch and
surrounding area.

The route itself starts from the other
end of the parking area, through a
walkers' gate with a footpath marker.
Cross the machair that lies beyond the
gate, keeping the fence on your left. This
curves right and then left before leading
down onto the sands of Traigh Bhi – yet
another magnificent Tiree beach. Turn
right to cross the sand to the far end and
then continue over the grass and rougher
ground above the shore. Aim for the ruins
of Patrick's Chapel – a low gable wall can
be seen set back above the coastline. This
isolated chapel dates from the 7th century
and contains two ancient stones carved
with crosses.

Keep following the coast, staying well
above the rocky inlets as the ground gets
increasingly rugged. From here you can
often make out the outline of the
Skerryvore Lighthouse on the horizon.

◄ View north from Beinn Ceann a'Mhara

The tallest lighthouse in Scotland, this elegant structure stands 48m high at a distance of more than 19km out to sea.

When you meet a fence, head uphill, keeping the fence and cliff edge on your left. The spectacular cliffs are awash with nesting seabirds in the summer months. Climb to the western summit of Ceann a' Mhara which is topped by a cairn and rewards the effort with great views northwards over Traig nan Gilean and Beinn Hough. From here head down into a gap before tackling the steady ascent up to the higher eastern summit of Beinn Ceann a'Mhara, an equally inspiring place to take a break.

From the top follow the fence southeast to reach a corner and then descend eastwards. This crosses rough ground at first before reaching the springy turf and flowers of the machair. Keep bearing east across the dunes and grass to return directly to the car park at the start.

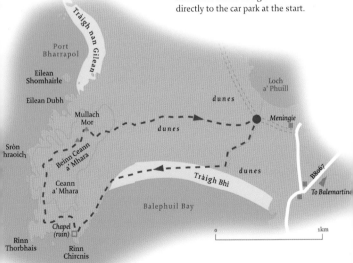

Hynish and Carnan Mor

Distance 8.25km Time 3 hours
Terrain pathless moor and grazing land,
some minor road Map OS Explorer 372
Access Calmac ferry from Oban, Ring-n-
Ride request bus on Tiree

Climb to the highest point on Tiree
before returning to the coast. The walk
begins from the Skerryvore Lighthouse
Signal Station buildings at Hynish,
which house a fascinating exhibition
and a café down at the pier.

Start from the parking area at the
Skerryvore exhibition building. The
complex of beautifully constructed stone
buildings is well worth exploring either at
the start or end of the walk. Restored by
the Hebridean Trust, Hynish was the site
of the signal station for the isolated
Skerryvore Lighthouse and the exhibition

tells the story of its construction and life.

Begin the walk by heading down to the
pier, constructed from huge blocks of
dressed stone, and pass in front of the old
pier store which is now converted to
provide group accommodation and a
seasonal café.

Go through the gate and bear right
across the grass to reach the signal tower.
From here messages were sent to
Skerryvore, the tallest and most isolated
of the Scottish lighthouses, which can
just be made out to the southwest in
clear weather. The lighthouse keepers'
cottages beyond the signal tower were
built in an unusual Egyptian style,
fashionable in Britain through the early
to mid-19th century. Return to the
parking area and then turn left along the
road, passing another building which

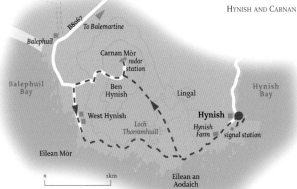

houses an exhibition on the Treshnish Isles, which lie between here and Mull and are a haven for birdlife.

After a gate the surfaced road becomes a track. Carry straight on, pass through another gate and stay on the now grassy track to reach a final house. Go through the gate here, passing the house to reach another gate and stile. Climb this and take the faint track leading along the shore, which can be boggy in places. Keep to the right of a rocky headland, staying on the springy turf and crossing the top of a green glen leading to the sea and known locally as 'Happy Valley'. Aim NNW to cross pathless moorland towards Carnan Mor. The summit is topped by a golf ball-like air traffic control radar station which makes it easy to keep in your sights.

The going gets rougher before a track leads northwest, passing through a gap in a drystane dyke onto the surfaced road. Turn right here to reach the summit. The trig point at the highest point is to the left, a short way from the ugly buildings.

The view is the real reason to make the climb; the Ceann a'Mhara headland can be seen to the west, with the flat croftland and beaches of Tiree stretching away to the north.

Descend using the road all the way to a junction near West Hynish. Turn left here to pass several houses, branching right to avoid the garden in front of the last cottage before continuing along the track to a gravel quarry by the coast. Avoid the quarry by keeping left and carry on across the grass, steering to the left of a concrete sheep fank. From a pebble bay the route back to Hynish stays above the rough coastline, remaining on the pathless higher ground to avoid the rocky bays and headlands below.

Eventually the route descends into the green sward of Happy Valley. Turn up this to rejoin the outward route, continuing round the coast and through the gates to the track after the first house and then the road back to Hynish.

◀ Hynish Pier

Index

Notes

Notes

Notes

Notes